IN GOD WE DO NOT TRUST

WALTER BRUEGGEMANN

EDITOR: CONRAD L. KANAGY

In God We Do Not Trust
by Walter Brueggemann
Editor: Conrad L. Kanagy

Copyright © 2024
All rights reserved.

Library of Congress Control Number: 2024943025
International Standard Book Number: 978-1-60126-941-6

SANTOS BOOKS

TO CAREY NEWMAN,
EXECUTIVE EDITOR OF FORTRESS PRESS

For giving more to both of us than he has any idea

TABLE OF CONTENTS

Editor's Introduction vii
Prologue ix

1. The Ten Commandments of MAGA 1
2. Peddlers of the Word 5
3. The Raw Power of Government 11
4. We the People 21
5. Two Kinds of Truth 30
6. The Father God Who Is No God-Father 39
7. The Empowering, Illuminating Word From Elsewhere 49
8. The Good Shepherd and the Bad Ones 55
9. The Dispossessing Power of Violent Greed 64
10. On Manning Up 75
11. A Revolution Hurried Along 84
12. Fear of the Unnumbered "Other" 92
13. Divine Genocide 102

Epilogue 112

EDITOR'S INTRODUCTION

This stirring series of essays by Walter Brueggemann represent the inaugural book for Santos Books. As with so many developments over the past four years, I awoke one morning with the idea of this press in my head. But like so many things that God does in our lives, the ground had long been prepared for its coming. A relationship and biography with Walter Brueggemann. Editorial mentoring by a patient and generous Carey Newman. My wife Heidi, who endured many experiments and through grace arrived at this moment with me.

The intent of this press is to be a place where saints can tell their stories. As a pastor I often referred to parishioners as "the saints." In typical Mennonite fashion, they usually denied being so. And sometimes they were correct. As Frederick Buechner likes to say, we are all both saints and sinners. But since "Saints and Sinners" Press is a cumbersome name for a publishing company, I will err on the side of assuming that within us all, sometimes hidden deep inside, lies a saint. Thus, Santos Books.

Who better than Walter Brueggemann to inaugurate this imprint? Sinner? Undoubtedly. Saint? By God's grace alone. Walter once told me that he is disliked by progressives because he still believes in that old formula, that it is by grace only that we are saved. And then he confided in me, "Conrad, I have to work to stay in that place of grace."

And I love that old truth. Work to stay in the place of grace. For without the work there is but cheap grace. But without the grace, the work matters not. And is ultimately, expensive work.

Each of these essays in this book poignantly speak to the crisis of the current American church. Decades ago, sociologist Robert Bellah warned us of the development of civil religion in America. The merging of God and country. The legitimization of country by God. The validation of war and violence and racism and abuse and oppression in the name of Christ. While Donald Trump may represent among the worst outcomes of this combination, he thrives on an existence that has been part of our country since the beginning.

As always, Brueggemann begins with the Bible and ends with the Bible. If your allegiance is to other than the Bible, you will find him offensive. But if your heart has been softened by the sword of the Spirit that lays bare the intents and motives of our souls, you will find in these essays great comfort.

Both Walter and Carey taught me that writing and publishing, while appearing veiled and obscure, are often simply the expression of sainthood that is within each of us. And when that story must come out—like from the bones of Jeremiah—where there's a will, there's a way.

If you have a story that you would like to share, the goal of this press is to make it possible for you to do so. No guarantees. No promises. But an openness to hear your story in a space and in a way that may not be possible in any other place or time. Email me at Kanagy.conrad@gmail.com.

June 2024

Conrad L. Kanagy, Ph.D.
Elizabethtown College

PROLOGUE

An Unending Governance

"What child is this who laid to rest on Mary's lap is sleeping?"
We ask in awe and wonder.
But wait!
We know who this child is:
We know: this is the child who will grow in authority to cast out demons,
> while we are beset by the demonic force of racism and nationalism.

We know: this is the child who will grow in capacity to feed the hungry multitudes,
> while we casually permit children all around the world to die of starvation.

We know: this is the child who will grow in power to heal the sick,
> while we are overrun with drug ads and quibble about deductions and co-payments.

We know: this is the child who will gain his life (and ours) by losing it.
This child, born to occupy center space in our lives, our energy, and our imagination,
> is the one who will dwell among us, full of grace and truth.

We know his name; we receive him as gift; we answer to his call to obedience.
This child, in his authority, capacity, and power, is the way of God among us.

> His governance shall have no end.

CHAPTER ONE

The Ten Commandments of MAGA

Over a decade ago, I drew from Exodus 5 the Ten Commandments of Pharaoh. All of them intend to compel more and more production.

1. Why are you taking the people away from their work? Get to your labors (v. 4)!
2. You shall no longer give the people straw to make bricks; let them go and gather straw for themselves (v. 7).
3. You shall require of them the same quantity of brick as they made previously; do not diminish it, for they are lazy (v. 8).
4. Let heavier work be laid on them; then they will labor at it and pay no attention to deceptive words (v. 9).
5. Go and get straw for yourselves, wherever you can find it; but your work will not be lessened in the least (v. 11).
6. Complete your work, the same daily assignment as when you were given straw (v. 13).
7. Why did you not finish the required quantity of bricks yesterday and today as you did before (v.14)?
8. You are lazy, lazy; that is why you say, "Let us go and sacrifice to the Lord" (v. 17).
9. Go now, and work; for no straw shall be given you, but you shall deliver the same number of bricks (v. 18).
10. You shall not lessen your daily number of bricks (v. 19).

The Ten Commandments that Moses received at Sinai were designed to contradict the commandments of Pharaoh, and to offer an astonishing alternative to the endless requirement of production. The Ten at Sinai intend to evoke a community of neighbors.

More recently I came across the Ten Commandments for the East German state articulated by Walter Ulbricht, the authoritarian leader of the state during the peak years of the Cold War. His Ten went like this:

1. Thou shalt always work toward the international solidarity of the proletariat and of all working people as well as for the inseparable bond of all socialist countries.

2. Thou shalt love thy country and always stand ready to use everything in your might and all your skill for the defence (sic) of the power of the workers and the peasants.

3. Thou shalt help to abolish the exploitation of the people by the people.

4. Thou shalt do good deeds for socialism, for socialism leads to a better life for all working people.

5. Thou shalt contribute to the build-up of socialism in the spirit of mutual help and comradely collaboration, respect for the collective and heed its critique.

6. Thou shalt protect the people's property and multiply it.

7. Thou shalt always strive for higher achievement, be frugal and consolidate the socialist work ethic.

8. Thou shalt raise your children in the spirit of peace and socialism to become well-rounded, confident and physically strong people.

9. Thou shalt live a clean and decent life and respect your family.

10. Thou shalt practice solidarity with the other peoples who fight for national liberty and defend their national independence (Katja Hoyer, *Beyond the Wall: A History of East Germany*, 2023, pp. 159-160).

After reflection on these decalogues, I thought it likely that one could imagine the Ten Commandments that might be issued for Donald Trump for his insurrectionist movement. This is what came to me:

1. Thou shalt heed only "Himself" and his changing whims.
2. Thou shalt bow down in loyalty only to "Himself," and to no other value or cause.
3. Thou shalt be free to use ugly, demeaning, and threatening language toward anyone else.
4. Thou shalt every day remain agitated and restless, ready for violence, and eager for revenge.
5. Thou shalt demean anyone who disagrees, including your parents.
6. Thou shalt use violent words and threatening actions that endanger the lives of others.
7. Thou shalt violate women as you may choose.
8. Thou shalt take whatever you want wherever you can get it.
9. Thou shalt lie as necessary, and so create an alternative universe.
10. Thou shalt covet and seize anything your neighbor may have, including his wife.

Given these several authorizations for an anti-neighborly life and culture, we are not unlike ancient Israel who stood in the Plains of Moab at the edge of the land of promise. It is no wonder that in that moment Moses issued an urgent either/or to his people of the covenant, an urgent imperative that pertains to us now:

> See, I have set before you today life and prosperity, death and adversity…Choose life so that you and your descendants may live (Deuteronomy 30:15, 19).

CHAPTER TWO

Peddlers of the Word

As is often the case with the Apostle Paul, he finds it necessary to make a defense of his apostolic ministry in II Corinthians 2. He insists that he is a person of sincerity sent by God who is, along with some others, "the aroma" of Christ. He contrasts himself to his opponents whom he dismisses as "peddlers of God's word," that is, as hucksters who are not to be trusted but who "corrupt" the gospel by mixing it with their self-interest. The word "peddler" drew my attention. It is the only usage of the term in the New Testament. It is used in the Greek translation of the Old Testament only in Isaiah 1:22 wherein, says the prophet, the wine of Israel is "mixed" with water and thereby diluted. We are not told much about Paul's opponents, but they clearly, in his judgment, had compromised the unalloyed good news of Jesus Christ.

The usage of the term "peddler" came to mind as I observed Donald Trump selling his "USA bible" for $59.99. I have not seen his Bible, but it clearly intends to voice the gospel alongside Trump's particular version of nationalism. As is always the case, the Bible in Trump's hands becomes simply another commodity whereby he can extend the reach of his shameless grifting. In the process, of course, the news of the gospel is completely distorted to serve his nefarious ends. Thus I had the notion that Trump, with his "USA Bible," is exactly the kind of peddler to which Paul alludes, who mixes, dilutes, and distorts the claims of the gospel for their own ends. Trump's sales pitch, in his never-ending quest for money, can appeal only to those who find the claims of the gospel too radical, or too free of ideology, who must therefore add to it an ideological slant that may reassure, but is no longer the gospel of Jesus Christ.

Alongside his Bible, Trump vowed to "make America pray again." He offered no suggestion about how he will "make" that happen. Nor does he seem to be aware that there is a vast company of believers ("vast" even in a time of retrenchment) who pray regularly, and who do not require his impetus for their practice of prayer. That good company of those who trust the gospel and who look to the Triune God as their source of life and wellbeing prays without ceasing.

WE PRAY FOR FORGIVENESS OF OUR SINS

> which we have sinned against you
> in thought, word, and deed,
> by what we have done,
> and by what we have left undone.
> We have not loved you with our whole heart;
> we have not loved our neighbor as ourselves.
> (*The Book of Common Prayer* 79)

The peddlers of course do not pray such prayers of confession, for they have no moral compass, and no sense that our lives are penultimate to and answerable to the holiness of God.

WE PRAY PRAYERS OF PETITION FOR OURSELVES.

We ask for attentive, transformative engagement with God in our weakness and in our strength, that we may be sustained in fullness of life, in obedience to God that is our true freedom. The peddlers of the word do not pray prayers of petition. Such peddlers of the word are capable of illusion, imagining that they have no needs, wants, or hopes to voice to God. Or, conversely, they do not imagine that there is a God of agency who can and will respond to our needs when they are acknowledged.

WE PRAY PRAYERS OF PETITION FOR OTHERS,

most especially for our loved ones and for neighbors in need who are disadvantaged and lacking adequate resources for life. The peddlers do not pray such prayers, because they do not have on their horizon any neighbors in need. They cannot entertain the thought that the needs of others might be a genuine concern for us.

WE PRAY PRAYERS OF THANKS

for the gifts of life and all the wonder of sustenance, maintenance, and support that come our way from the generous hand of God. The peddlers do not pray such prayers of gratitude because they do not know that there is an ultimate Giver of good gifts. Indeed, they think that there are no gifts given. There are only achievements and accomplishments, and advantages gained by careful, shrewd, or ruthless dealing.

Thus when Mr. Trump proposes to "make America pray again," his intent will not be prayers of *confession*, of *petition*, of *intercession*, or of *thanks*; that does not leave much. Of course he does not specify the content of his prayers, but they may be prayers for the advancement of his nationalist, racist, misogynist agenda. He and other peddlers would find it incomprehensible to affirm with an answer from 101 in *The Evangelical Catechism*:

> Prayer is the conversation of the heart with God for the purpose of praising him, asking him to supply the needs of ourselves and others, and thanking him for whatever he gives us.

Or the answer in *The Heidelberg Catechism* to question 116:

> Why is prayer necessary for Christians?
>
> Because it is the chief part of the gratitude which God requires of us, and because God will give his grace and Holy Spirit only to those who sincerely beseech him in prayer without ceasing, and who thank him for these gifts.

The peddlers, Mr. Trump among them, are the practitioners of the ruthless kind of cynicism that aims to exploit the cadences of faith in their drive for money and power. This practice of cynicism, moreover, can readily evoke a response of repulsion from those who reject the grifting. Thus it is important for the community of the faithful, those who regularly pray prayers of confession, petition, intercession, and thanks, to refuse the cynicism to which we are menacingly invited. It is important to maintain a "second naiveté" of innocent trust in the Giver of all good gifts. We may pay particular attention to the answer of *The Heidelberg Catechism* to question 120 concerning why the Lord's Prayer addresses God as "father":

> That at the very beginning of our prayer he may awaken in us the childlike reverence and trust toward God which should be the motivation of our prayer, which is that God has become our Father through Christ and will much less deny us what we ask him in faith than our human fathers will refuse us earthly things.

This answer of course is cast in patriarchal terms. But it need not be. It can as well be expressed in maternal images as the good Mother God who does not deny what we ask any more than our human mothers refuse us earthly things.

Trump's crass distortion of our faith—with reference to both the Bible and to the practice of prayer—can amount to a compelling summons to the ministry of the church. It can remind us why we must insist, in every season, that the community of the faithful is quite distinct from and counter to the ideological passion of hucksters who tend to prey rather than pray. It may remind us that our practice of prayer is not incidental to our faith, but it is at the heart of our daily acknowledgement that we live from, rely on, and gladly respond to the Giver of all gifts. I suspect that in many congregations we have work to do to teach the faithful how to pray more faithfully. There is, on the one hand, the seduction of rote reiteration of prayers that can be done without much thinking or intentionality. On the other hand, there is a temptation to keep our prayers politely on the surface of our lives without the expression of our deepest failures or our deepest needs, our deepest hopes, and our deepest fears.

The final question on prayer in *The Evangelical Catechism* is "Are all our prayers answered?" The answer:

> All prayers are answered either in the way we expect God to answer them, or in the way God knows will be best for us.

This answer bespeaks a profound trust in the goodness of God, a deep expectation that God's intention will prevail in the world, with a readiness to trust, in hope, in the goodness of God. No deep imagination is required to see how completely this stance contradicts the world of the peddlers.

The conclusion is that the good news is not for sale. It is not a commodity. It will not, in faithfulness, be distorted for the sake of our favorite ideologies. It is, itself, the real thing, the real truth of our lives. This is a time for the church to voice its deepest truth bravely and clearly. I write this on Maundy Thursday when we ponder the suffering and death of the Messiah who will be raised in power. Such a claim boldly refuses every distortion and every convenient ideology. This is a time for brave testimony that is unembarrassed and uncompromising.

So much for "Two Corinthians"!

CHAPTER THREE

The Raw Power of Government

My purpose in wring this brief piece is to invite you to dwell for a time with *Psalm 72*, to listen to it closely for a day or for this week. At the outset we may recognize two matters concerning the Psalm. First, you will notice that the Psalm stands in the final position in Book II of the Psalter, as though it were the finale and grand conclusion of this set of Psalms. As a "royal Psalm" (one pertaining to the life of the king), it may be strategically placed as an assurance of viable governance. Book II begins with Psalm 42 and includes a number of lament Psalms. But by Psalm 72, the collection has moved beyond grief to responsible governance.

Second, the Psalm by tradition (fictively!) is addressed to King Solomon. This is important because its advocacy of restorative justice is addressed to the king who, in the tradition, most fully participates in predatory covetousness. Thus the Psalm proposes an ethic and an economic practice that is to counter the excesses of royal greed.

The pattern of the Psalm is an alteration between two themes. On the one hand the Psalm, in a repeated optative cadence, hopes and expects that *royal governance will prosper*. Thus in verses 5-7 it is hoped and expected that the king and his realm will be as generative as rain showers, so that peace (*shalom*) may abound. In verses 8-11 it is anticipated that the king will govern the entire known world from Spain (Tarshish) to Arabia, so that kings will serve him, and bring their wealth to him as tribute. See the case of the queen of Sheba in I Kings 10:1-10:

> Then she gave the king one hundred twenty talents of gold, a great quantity of spices, and precious stones; never again did spices come in such quantity as that which the queen of Sheba gave to King Solomon (v. 10).

The same anticipatory sentiment is voiced in the more familiar words of the prophet Isaiah:

> His authority will grow continually,
> and there shall be endless peace
> for the throne of David and his kingdom (Isaiah 9:7).

The older, more familiar translation concerns "the increase of his government," that is, the extent of his rule will continue to expand, assuring luxurious wellbeing.

The theme is reiterated in verses I Kings 10:15-17. Again there is "the gold of Sheba" plus abundant grain and durable fame. This theme that dominates the Psalm is a liturgic assurance (guarantee?) that concerns the longevity, wellbeing, and prosperity of the ruling house. It is not difficult to imagine this Psalm being voiced in the Jerusalem temple in the presence of the royal house. It was perhaps on an occasion when the claims of the dynasty were renewed and reiterated amid the glad celebrative mood of those admitted to the liturgy and to the generosity of the regime.

But this glad affirmation has as its counterpoint a second theme that brings royal attention back to the facts on the ground, namely, *the economic reality of poor people who lack resources for life.* Thus in verses 2 and 4, this royal liturgy places the poor and needy before the king, and assigns to the king the role of advocate against the power of aggressive accumulation:

> May he judge your people with righteousness,
> and your poor with justice…
> May he defend the cause of the poor of the people,
> and give deliverance to the needy,
> and crush the oppressor (Psalm 72:2, 4).

It is as though the Psalm not only recognized the reality of an aggressive economic system, but also noticed that the king himself might be a party to that oppressive system. But no, not this king! This king belongs on the side of the poor and vulnerable.

The theme is reiterated in verses 12-14:

> For he delivers the needy when they call,
> the poor and those who have no helper.
> He has pity on the weak and the needy,
> and saves the lives of the needy.
> From oppression and violence he redeems their life;
> and precious is their blood in his sight (Psalm 72:12-14).

The king is assigned the role of advocate when the vulnerable have "no helper." The roster of those who rely on the king's help includes the weak, the poor, and the needy. Royal power is to be invested against violent systems of oppression. It is the real work of a "redeemer" to rescue and restore those exploited by a predatory economic system. The liturgic articulation is of course poetic. It does not specify the concrete economic actions to be undertaken, but clearly the king is summoned to do something like reparations in order to restore the dignity, security, and viability of those lost in the shuffle of systemic greed.

The Psalm moves easily back and forth from one theme to the other. It does not in any specific way indicate how the two themes are related to each other. It is surely credible, nonetheless, to conclude that these rich scenarios of royal prosperity are related to care for the economically vulnerable as *effect* to cause. It is exactly royal engagement with the poor, weak, and needy that makes possible the flourishing that the Psalm anticipates. The reason the two parts are so linked, moreover, is that the creator God has intended, in every season, that social power should be devoted to and invested in a community of neighbors who are all together in one network of well-being. No one can opt out of the network, certainly not the king. No one can for long monopolize resources against the needs and requirements of the community. Thus this liturgic piece maps out for the royal entourage and its adherents the insistent connections that are engrained in the very structure of creation.

In the long recital of kings in the Old Testament, it is King Josiah, near the end of the dynastic line, who seems to have most understood this ingrained connection that helps to curb, direct, and propel royal responsibility. In the narrative report on King Josiah and his reform, it is stated that he destroyed all the *iconography of the foreign gods* (II Kings 23:4-15). That is all. In context, however, we may recognize that it is the religious icons that gave legitimacy to systemic policies and practices of greed. Thus Josiah's actions worked to destroy the legitimating power that propelled the greed that victimized the weak, poor, and needy. It is reported, moreover, that King Josiah reinstituted the *Passover*, as though to make his domain an exodus-remembering, exodus-practicing enterprise. Josiah, beyond that, reinstituted the *covenant* that helped to bind all together, rich and poor, weak and strong, needy and well-positioned, all as neighbors:

> The king went up to the house of the Lord, and with him went all the people of Judah, all the inhabitants of Jerusalem, the priests, the prophets, and all the people, both small and great; he read in their hearing all the words of the book of the covenant that had been found in the house of the Lord. The king stood by the pillar and made a covenant before the Lord, to follow the Lord, keeping his commandments, his decrees, and his statutes, with all his heart and all his soul, to perform the words of this covenant that were written in this book. All the people joined in the covenant (II Kings 23:2-3).

Josiah did nothing less than redefine and reorder the public life of Israel according to the old covenantal traditions of the book of Deuteronomy with its accent on care for the widow, orphan, and immigrant. In this way the king bound together the *biggest royal hopes of the Psalm* and the *most rigorous requirements of the Torah*.

The matter is given succinct articulation by Jeremiah who contrasted father Josiah with his rapacious royal son, Jehoiakim (Shallum) (Jeremiah 22:11-19). Of Josiah, the king who reconstituted the public life of Israel, the prophet could declare:

> Did not your father eat and drink
> and do justice and righteousness?
> Then it was well with him.
> He judged the cause of the poor and needy;
> then it was well.
> Is not this to know me? says the Lord (Jeremiah 22:15-16).

The terms of the Psalm are all there:

> justice and righteousness;
> poor and needy;
> the double use of "well" (tov).

José Miranda, *Marx and the Bible*, can write of these verses:

> Yahweh is not among the entities nor the existings nor in univocal being nor in analogous being, but rather in the implacable moral imperative of justice (49).

The connection of these two themes of the Psalm is unmistakably in this rendering of the belated king. It is the business of government to redress the economic injustices that have been perpetrated. The future wellbeing of the Jerusalem establishment depends upon it!

The teachable, preachable point of Psalm 72, I suggest, is the *non-negotiable linkage* of just restoration for the vulnerable and societal wellbeing (and eventually environmental wellbeing). This linkage is elemental to the claims of covenant and prophetic tradition. And when that linkage is violated or disregarded, big trouble comes. It comes not only to the vulnerable who suffer where there is a failure of restorative justice. It comes also to the moneyed, the powerful, and the well-positioned, because privileged wellbeing is not sustainable in the long run. The way the Old Testament works is to show that when the power structure of old Jerusalem rejected the proper claims of the vulnerable, big disturbance came. It may come in many forms, but it cannot finally be resisted or averted because, so the tradition insists, God's creation is coherently and morally ordered. Those who seek to outflank that order are, in the Psalter, termed "fools":

> Fools say in their hearts,
> "There is no God."
> They are corrupt; they do abominable deeds;
> There is no one who does good (Psalm 14:1).

They do not say this out loud, but only in their secret thinking and scheming. Theirs is not a frontal denial of God, or a theoretical atheism. This is, rather, *practical atheism* that imagines there is no moral reckoning or limit to created reality. This "atheism" is performed by "abominable deeds" (v. 1). Specifically:

> Have they no knowledge, all the evildoers
> who eat up my people as they eat bread,
> and do not call on the Lord (v. 4)?

Such "fools" seek to "confound the plans of the poor" (v. 6). The governance of the Creator, however, tells otherwise. The impact of his connection must have been sobering to the self-absorbed regime in ancient Jerusalem. It might, in like manner, be sobering now among us when the connection is made visible and compelling.

I have pondered Psalm 72 amid a church across our land where almost every church member is zealous and generous about charity, with a will to ameliorate social vexations. The same church, for the most part, is indifferent to and uninterested in the capacity of government to invest in serious and significant social betterment and transformation. The reason Psalm 72 might be an important reference point for us now is that it insists that it is exactly the proper role of government (so Solomon) with its great resources to be in the business of equitable economic justice for the vulnerable and the disempowered. It is the work of the church, in such a frame of reference, to insist that the government do its proper work. This insistence, of necessity, opposes any "small government" mantra of the privileged who want there to be no interference with their easier private economic wealth. This issue must be joined, not because any of us is a "bleeding heart liberal," but because government is understood, in important strands of our faith, as an instrument of God's restorative justice.

All the while I was pondering this Psalm I had ringing in my ears the phrasing of Arianna Huffington from long ago. I have only a brief exact phrase from her. She said, in general, that private charity is good for the support of the symphony and the opera; but when it comes to needy children, we need "the raw power of government." This is her phrasing and it is exactly correct. The "raw power of government" has the resources and the clout to make a difference. In the Psalm the kings are urged to use "the raw power of government" on behalf of the weak, the poor, and the needy. In this Psalm this is more than an urging. It is recognition that such rescue of the weak, needy, and poor from the hand of the "oppressor" is a condition for societal and environmental wellbeing.

According to this Psalm, the government (Solomon, kingship) has a chance to flourish. All it has to do is to execute its mandate toward the weak, poor, and needy. All it had to do was exercise "raw power" for its most important subjects. But of course they did not:

> Yet the Lord warned Israel and Judah by every prophet and every seer, saying, "Turn from your evil ways and keep my commandments and my statutes, in accordance with all the law that I commanded your ancestors and that I sent to you by my servants the prophets." They would not listen but were stubborn, as their ancestors had been, who did not believe in the Lord their God. They despised his statutes, and his covenant that he made with their ancestors, and the warnings that he gave them (II Kings 17:13-15).

And so the Psalter moves along from Psalm 72 until we come to Psalm 89, the concluding Psalm of Book III, yet another royal Psalm. In Psalm 89, Davidic kingship (the family of Solomon!) is celebrated for its reliance on and practice of covenantal fidelity:

> I declare that your steadfast love is established forever;
> your faithfulness is as firm as the heavens...
> Righteousness and justice are the foundation of your throne;

> steadfast love and faithfulness go before you…
> My faithfulness and steadfast love shall be with him;
> and in my name his horn shall be exalted…
> But I will not remove from him my steadfast love,
> or be false to my faithfulness (Psalm 89:2, 14, 24, 33).

But then, alas! In verses 38-51, the reality of covenantal faithfulness has vanished:

> Lord, where is your steadfast love of old,
> which by your faithfulness you swore to David? (Psalm 89:49)

God's steadfast love vanished from a regime that could not do its proper work. Thus Psalm 89 is a reality check on the hopes of Psalm 72. Nevertheless, Psalm 72 continues to voice hope. It keeps hoping on behalf of every new king, every new regime, and every new government. It hopes that the "raw power of government" will be faithfully and fully deployed on behalf of the poor, the weak, and the needy. It is the proper work of government in a world where the creator God presides. We are not finished in our commentary concerning "the raw power of government" until we do such a reality check of actual practice. Thus Psalm 89 is a crucial cognate to Psalm 72.

But then, a sober counter-thought, alas! I write this in the wake of the court's revocation of Roe v. Wade. In that court action we are watching the "raw power of government" being deployed against the bodies of women and the future of women. Of course we know that the "raw power of government" can be wrongly performed for nefarious ends. John Calvin, my place of rootage, had a very high view of government and urged that even bad government must be honored and obeyed. On the final page of his *Institutes*, however, Calvin offers a decisive caveat to his general commitment to government:

> We may not be submissive to the corrupt desires of men, much less be slaves to their impiety (*Institutes of the Christian Religion II* [Philadelphia: Presbyterian Board of Christian Education]) (806).

Calvin quotes Acts 5:29, "We must obey God rather than men." A few pages earlier he writes:

> All laws are preposterous which neglect the claims of God, and merely provide for the interests of men (779-80).

Calvin uses the term "men" conventionally and uncritically. In our own context, however, we may see that it is exactly "men" who sponsor and who underwrite such court actions that do great damage to vulnerable women. It is nothing less than a *forceful return of patriarchy*! We are witnesses to the energy of "the raw power of government" deployed against vulnerable women to shameful ends.

The lyrical imagination of Psalm 72 soars beyond the close reasoning of Calvin. But they come to the same point. The raw power of government is to be used *on behalf of the vulnerable*, not against them. It is a sad occasion when the "magistrates" (Calvin's preferred term) act against the vulnerable. The kings in ancient Israel learned the hard way:

> Judah also did not keep the commandments of the Lord their God but walked in the customs that Israel had introduced. The Lord rejected all the descendents of Israel; he punished them and gave them into the hand of plunderers, until he had banished them from his presence (II Kings 17:19-20).

We know better than that; and we can act more covenantally than did they.

CHAPTER FOUR

We the People

The Gospel of Luke places an acute social conflict at the center of his gospel narrative. In the episode of "the cleansing of the temple," Luke juxtaposes the two parties to the conflict that runs through the narrative (Luke 19:45-48):

- **The chief priests, scribes, and leaders of the people.** These are the urban elite who clustered around the temple, symbol of religious and political unity and tax-collecting apparatus.

versus

- **The people**, those who were "spellbound" by the teaching of Jesus.

It is a very old, long-running conflict between elites who feared change "from below" and those eager for change because they knew they were presently denied their rightful share of the bounty of the community. Luke of course places Jesus at the center of the dispute, the one whose very life *constitutes a threat* to the monopoly of the elites and whose very life *constitutes an alternative possibility* for the disadvantaged. In the end, the elites would prevail via their execution of Jesus as an enemy of the regime. In the end, that is…except that the narrative does not end with the Friday of execution.

In Matthew's telling of the same incident the dispute concerns the "blind and lame" whom he healed, and an index of "amazing things" he performed that defied the settled world of the "chief priests and scribes" (Matthew 21:14-15). The rendering in Mark 11:15-19 offers the same language as Luke, but the opposition is described differently as "chief priests and scribes" versus "the whole crowd." The narratives are consistent in their conclusion that what *frightened the privileged* was what was utterly *compelling to the mass of people* who lived amid an exploitative socio-political-religious environment. His presence and his actions that defied conventional explanation in the eyes of the disadvantaged made possible what had seemed to them to be impossible. The healing of the blind and lame was verification of his capacity to work effectively outside of conventional norms for the sake of wellbeing.

We may pause to reflect on the population of these disadvantaged folk who are designated as "the people" (*laos*) or "the whole crowd" (*oxlos*). This mass of people is recurringly the subject matter of the biblical narrative, even though the elites seek to exclude this same population from access, influence, or empowerment. If we look long term at the formation of such a population, we may reach back to the phrasing of Exodus 12:38 where the mass of people enroute to the wilderness is designated as '*rv rav* that NRSV translates as "mixed crowd":

> A *mixed crowd* also went up with them, and livestock in great numbers, both flocks and herds. They baked unleavened cakes of the dough that they had brought out of Egypt; it was not leavened, because they were driven out of Egypt and could not wait, nor had they prepared any provisions for themselves (Exodus 12:38-39).

This company enroute to the wilderness was without pedigree or tribal identity. That company lacked any cohesion beyond the fact that they had escaped "were driven out of" Egypt, and were on the run without "any provisions for themselves" (v. 39).

We may entertain the thought that the Bible narrates the process whereby that "*mixed crowd*" without any identity was transformed into a "*holy people*." When we reach belatedly Nehemiah 13:3, it is Israel as a "holy people" who is separated from all those of "foreign descent" (*col-'rv*). The transformation from "no people" to "holy people" is accomplished by the wonder, power, and will of YHWH:

> Now therefore, if you obey my voice and keep my covenant, you shall be my treasured possession out of all the peoples. Indeed the whole earth is mine, but you shall be for me a priestly kingdom and a holy nation (Exodus 19:5-6).

God makes covenant with this mixed multitude, imposes commandments on them, and bestows a peculiar role and identity on them. This "holy people" bears all the marks of a "mixed crowd" and is never characterized by any pedigree of its own. Their new identity is all by the will of this "people-making" God. Indeed Hosea can go so far as to imagine that this people can forfeit its status and become "no people:"

> Then the Lord said, "Name him *Lo-ammi*, for you are not my people and I am not your God (Hosea 1:9).

To be sure, Hosea promptly reverses field so that God reconstitutes this no-people as God's people:

> I will have pity on *Lo-ruhamah*,
> and I will say to *Lo-ammi*,
> "You are my people";
> and he will say, "You are my God" (Hosea 2:23).

Both the ending and the restoration of this people are all at the behest of YHWH.

The matter is not different concerning "the people" in the New Testament:

> But you are a chosen race, a royal priesthood, a holy nation, God's own people, in order that you may proclaim the mighty acts of him who called you out of darkness into his marvelous light.
>
> Once you were not a people,
> but now you are God's people;
> once you had not received mercy,
> but now you have received mercy (I Peter 2:9-10).

It is the gift of mercy that transposes a *"no-people"* into a *people* with an historical presence and destiny!

If we have this memory of "people-making" in purview, we might notice in the episode of temple cleansing in the Gospel narrative that Jesus is indeed at work forming a 'people' who are gathered around his inexplicable power to make new. This people (*laos*), that is, the whole crowd (*oxlos*), eagerly responded to the possibilities he generated, because they knew for certain that present social arrangements governed by "the chief priests and scribes" were for them a dead end. There is no prospect for ever gaining wellbeing, influence, or power in the present system. They are for good reason "spellbound" by his possibilities beyond all present impossibilities.

We should notice, however, that the elites (chief priests and scribes) did everything they could to maintain their own control and their exclusive access to wealth and wellbeing. In the temple system of ancient Israel, the primary strategy for such exclusion was the "purity codes" that effectively eliminated access to all those "unlike us."

Thus the temple itself had gradations of holiness for which selected groups of people had various levels of access.

And now in our own turn in our own time the "holy people," that is, the ones of European extraction, are competent to devise tools of exclusion for all others in order to protect advantage. Such tools are variously in the service of segregation signaled by familiar phrases:

> We reserve the right to refuse service…
> No xxx need apply.

The strategy applies to immigration policy as well as restrictions in housing, schools, transport, and health services. The elite in Jesus' time would have claimed to be protecting "holiness" by their exclusionary temple practices. The gospel narrative constitutes a dramatic articulation of Jesus' solidarity with those excluded. Thus with reference to Mark 12:41-44, yet another confrontation enacted in the temple, Allan Boesak, *Dare We Speak of Hope? Searching for a Language of Life in Faith and Politics* (2014) can write:

> When Mark writes that Jesus stations himself "opposite" the temple treasury, he is not talking space and position. He is talking *opposition*: opposition to exploitation, to abuse of the faith of the poor, to the false piousness that proffers avarice as devotion to God. No, it is not sentimental approval of baptized exploitation we are seeing here—it is divine outrage. The temple tax system that made riches for the temple elite made victims of the poor. Jesus knew what the people needed was to be freed from the awe of the temple, the temple system, and the power of the ruling elite so that they might be free from the paralyzing fear of offending God by rejecting the caretakers of God's supposed house (64).

The very ones whom the elite seek to exclude are the primary candidates to constitute the community of Jesus, for the "holy people" is formed "from below" among those who live a distance from the mirages of virtue and control.

All of this was on my mind as I read *Globalists: The End of Empire and the Birth of Neoliberalism* by Quinn Slobodian (2018). Slobodian details the way in which neoliberal ideology and practice have displaced the force of empire and its colonization. He takes the trouble to list elements of "a basic consensus" among neoliberals, notably those of the "Geneva School." Among the fifteen notes of consensus that he articulates, two in particular bear upon this discussion:

> *#6 Democracy is a potential threat to the functioning of the market order. Therefore, safeguards against the disruptive capacity of democracy are necessary.*
> *#7 Democracy's danger is its legitimation of demands for redistribution. All world economic problems are rooted in domestic distribution struggles* (p. 272).

In this telling, democracy constitutes a threat to an unfettered market order because *the wrong kind of people* may have a voice in financial affairs. Through this perspective I have come to understand in fresh ways why we have among us all kinds of restrictions to democracy, variously expressed through gerrymandering and voter repression. Such efforts occur because *the wrong kind of people* may intrude upon the unfettered gains of the powerful and moneyed. Thus the curtailment of democracy in our contemporary context is equivalent to Israel's old purity codes that serve to prevent *the wrong kind of people* from gaining access or influence. It is exactly *the wrong kind of people* who were spellbound by Jesus and who flocked to him to form God's "new people" in the world, the carriers of God's newness that shows up as merciful justice.

Proposition #7 in the list by Slobodian is even more poignant. The great fear of democracy—with the wrong kind of people having a voice—concerns *redistribution of community resources*. Such a force of democracy does not arise from any formal commitment to "socialism" or any other ideology. It is rather simply an insistence that the resources of the community must be devoted to the wellbeing of the community, its health care, its schools, its transport, and its housing. Of course such redistribution via taxation contradicts our regnant ideology of greed that justifies great private wealth at the expense of the common good. That is exactly what was at stake in the gospel narrative in which the "chief priests and scribes" managed public funds to their own advantage. The "woe oracles" of Jesus in Matthew 23 are precisely to the point of such abuse of public power for private gain.

> Woe to you, scribes and Pharisees, hypocrites! For you tithe mint, dill, and cummin, and have neglected the weightier matters of the law: justice and mercy and faith. (Matthew 23:23).

The antidote to such mechanizations, as Slobodian sees clearly, is that the *demos* (the people-*laos-oxlos*) should have access and power to enact public possibility. Thus Jesus is on the side of the *demos* who are mesmerized by the possibilities Jesus exhibits outside the norms of official order.

It is worth a pause to consider the kind of "order" that the "mixed crowd" might fashion for the management of the public good. We might well look to Israel's Torah for clues about an alternative economic order as the "mixed crowd" convened at Sinai. Out of the Sinai confrontation came guidance for social reconstruction, at the center of which is a requirement for debt cancellation in the "Year of Release" (Deuteronomy 15:1-18) and the Jubilee Year

(Leviticus 25). There can be no doubt that debt is a primary tool of neoliberalism, as the financial community imposes its insatiable demands on the vulnerable, placing them in hopeless debt and so reducing them to cheap labor. (See David Graeber, *Debt: The First 5,000 Years*).Conversely the Torah provisions permitted those in debt to "begin again" with debt cancelled, to reenter the economy in viable ways. Of course, what spellbound the crowds around Jesus was his empowerment of vulnerable people to begin again, forgiven, healed, restored, and rejoicing. That is the will of the Torah and the offer of the Gospel.

In truth the church has too readily been on the wrong side of this defining question of shared wellbeing all too often. Too often the church has echoed and legitimated the interests of the moneyed. The church has had two theological strategies for such a misguided illusion. First, we have *spiritualized and privatized* our sense of salvation, thus easily supporting the most mistaken individualism at the expense of the common good. Second, we have much too much emphasized *life-after-death* and *other-worldliness* that took away energy from the urgency of justice and mercy in this present world. The antidote for the church of course is to accent its *this-world* care for the neighborhood, and its *communitarian conviction* that as neighbors we are all in it together.

At the center of this-world engagement is a readiness for *redistribution* of common resources and allocation of funds for the neediest of neighbors. The church's insistence, at every turn, on this-world community will go far to escape the easy religious temptation of privatized individualism and other-worldly escapism. All we need is to engage seriously the covenantal-prophetic traditions of the Torah (the ones downplayed in the common lectionary) to understand the vortex in which Jesus was formed, by which he was instructed, and to which he bore steady witness. It is always about the people, about the ordinary folk who do not have great resources but who have names to honor, lives to protect, and identities to preserve. Our faith concerns the mass of folk who clustered around Jesus spellbound.

The religious orientation of Abraham Lincoln is most elusive. There can be no doubt, however, that his stunning formulation in his Gettysburg Address is exactly to the point. Our common faith and our common political requirement is a governance,

> of the people,
> by the people, and
> for the people.

It is the rule of the demos (*laos, oxlos*), democracy. That rule is under threat from the force of neoliberalism that has largely preempted the tools of government. For good reason Slobodian ends his important book with this stunning sentence:

> In the mid-2010s, the popular referendum in favor of Brexit and the declining popularity of binding trade legislation suggest that even if the intention of the neoliberals was to "undo the demos," the demos—for better or worse—is not undone yet (286).

A great deal is at stake in this for our society, and thus for the church in its calling to speak the truth to the people of the power of money.

CHAPTER FIVE

Two Kinds of Truth

My favorite detective writer is Michael Connelly with his torrent of books concerning detective Harry Bosch and his half-brother, Mickey Haller, the Lincoln Lawyer. In his book of 2017, *Two Kinds of Truth*, Connelly has Bosch chasing down, at great risk to his life, a ruthless drug ring. Bosch is accused of planting evidence in order to convict an alleged killer. But his several colleagues and his several nemeses in law enforcement miscalculate about him. The narrator declares:

> What Kennedy, Soto, and Tapscott could not know was what Bosch knew in the deepest, darkest part of his heart. That he had not planted evidence against Borders. That he had never planted evidence against any suspect or adversary in his life. And this knowledge gave Bosch an affirming jolt of adrenalin and purpose. He knew there were two kinds of truth in this world. The truth that was the unalterable bedrock of one's life and mission. And the other, malleable truth of politicians, charlatans, corrupt lawyers, and their clients, bent and molded to serve whatever purpose was at hand (128).

The story that unfolds here is the truth of the incorruptible Bosch, and his cunning enemies in law enforcement.

Much later in the story Bosch's daughter, Maddie, gently reprimands her father for taking what seem to be outrageous risks in his sense of duty. To his daughter, Bosch responds:

> Look, I'm sorry. But I wanted to catch these guys. What that kid did, the son, it was noble. When all this comes out, people will probably say he was stupid and naive and didn't know what he was doing. But they won't know the truth. He was being noble. And there isn't a lot of that out there in the world anymore. People lie, presidents lie, corporations lie and cheat… The world is ugly and not many people are willing to stand up to it anymore. I didn't want what this kid did to go by without… I didn't want them to get away with it, I guess. (289).

Bosch explains to his daughter that he acted in risky ways in order to settle scores on behalf of an innocent kid who was ruthlessly gunned down by the drug syndicate.

This reflective commentary by Bosch got me to thinking about "two kinds of truth," the phrasing around which Connelly frames his thriller. There is the easy, compromised truth of ruthless, powerful people who can mostly act with impunity, and there is the "unalterable bedrock" truth that Bosch in his practice fully embraces and embodies. It is such faithful practice that upholds justice, and beyond justice, assures human dignity and wellbeing. This framing by Connelly via Bosch got me to thinking about how "two kinds of truth" show up, recurringly, in the Bible.

At the very outset, we get these "two kinds of truth" in the Exodus narrative. The truth with which Pharaoh operates in his predatory impatience is (a) that he needs more bricks with which to store his surplus wealth, and (b) that his Hebrew slaves are "lazy." His truth deals in quantification, and has no interest in or capacity to notice the reality of human suffering, pain, or weariness evoked by his brick quotas. By contrast, the truth carried by the Hebrew slaves and thus by Moses is a truth closely embedded in their bodies. Thus they "groaned and cried out" (Exodus 2:23). They did not groan about the number of bricks. Nor did they cry out because of the regimen of work. Rather, their "groan and cry out" was about the truth they knew best, that their bodies could not pay the cost of sustaining Pharaoh's quantification. Eventually they had to run the risk of departure from Pharaoh in order to honor the unbearable truth of their bodies. It is recurringly the case that Pharaoh and his company— politicians, charlatans, corrupt lawyers—did not and could not know that the pain of slave bodies was a truth with which they had to reckon. The contest of "two kinds of truth," moreover, is kicked upstairs, so that the Egyptian gods are patrons of quantity, whereas YHWH, the covenantal God summoned to the slave camp by bodily pain, is attentive to another truth: "God heard, God remembered, God looked, God took notice" (Exodus 2:24-25). This is the God who will not avert eyes away from bodily truth.

The same struggle between "two kinds of truth" is defining in the Elijah-Elisha narratives. The confrontation between "two truths" is dramatically joined in the contest at Mt. Carmel wherein Baal is a patron of the royal establishment of Omri, Ahab, and Jezebel (I Kings 18). YHWH, by contrast, is the advocate for the peasant Israelites who live a subsistence life. The dramatic either/or of Mt. Carmel is on full exhibit in the narrative of I Kings 21 concerning Naboth's vineyard. In that narrative, King Ahab's truth of possessiveness takes land as a fungible commodity. By contrast, Naboth, the subsistence peasant, knows land to be intimately linked to his family and to his identity in relational ways. In the short run, the commoditizing thought of Ahab prevails. In the long run, of course, that royal self-deceit cannot prevail against the insistent relationality of land and identity. (NB how immediately pertinent is this narration to the White-Europeans land seizure of Native American land where the blood continues to cry out from the ground.)

In the stunning Elisha narratives the conflict between "two kinds of truth" is played out with specificity:

- In II Kings 5 Elisha adroitly heals the bodily disease of the Syrian general, while the Israelite king is helpless before such suffering (see II Kings 5:7).
- In II Kings 6:8-24 the intent of the Syrian king is foiled, as is the desire of the Israelite king to kill his enemies. In the face of these two failed kings, the truth of Elisha prevails that is his will for peace:

And the Arameans no longer came raiding in the land of Israel (6:23).

- In the narrative concerning an acute famine, II Kings 6:24-7:20, we notice at the outset the king's inability to respond usefully to the hungry woman:

No! Let the Lord help you. How can I help you? From the threshing floor or from the winepress? (v. 27)

By contrast to the king, Elisha promises food to the woman, food that is wondrously provided at the end of the narrative.

In each of these narratives we observe that royal truth cannot deliver anything useful, while the royal house continued to bask in its power and wealth. By contrast, Elisha, who had neither wealth nor power, can and does deliver transformative aid in the interest of bodily wellbeing.

It is no surprise that the alternative truth carried by Moses, Elijah, and Elisha turns up decisively in the narratives of Jesus. Indeed Luke succinctly summarizes the dispute, tension, and contradiction between these two kinds of truth:

> Every day he was teaching in the temple. The chief priests, the scribes, and the leaders of the people kept looking for a way to kill him; but they did not find anything they could do, for all the people were spellbound by what they heard (Luke 19:47-48).

The urban power structure in Jerusalem—chief priests, scribes, leaders—specialized in official truth. They made the rules, kept the rules, and interpreted the rules. And they saw, repeatedly, that Jesus readily overstepped the rules in terms of generative, transformative power. They rightly reasoned that he had to be stopped, or the entire structure of control would be exposed and defeated. It was no wonder that they "kept looking for a way to execute him" as a violator of their truth. Everything in Luke's summary turns on the adversative conjunction in verse 8, "but." What follows that conjunction is a complete contrast to the foregoing. "The people," the nameless throng without power, wealth, or resources, flocked to his exhibit of restorative transformative power. They found his teaching as compelling as his actions. They were "spellbound" by what he said to them. And what he said to them was a portrayal of an alternative social possibility that was not top-down. That prospect of alternative governance represents, recurringly, a profound threat to establishment power and its claim of truth. Thus "the people" had no doubt that Jesus, in his words and in his actions, evidenced a truth that was not accountable to the governing establishment and not answerable to its truth.

Thus everywhere in scripture the issue is joined between these two kinds of truth. One truth is *top-down*. It originates in and serves the aims of established power. It tends to be quantifiable, provides certitude and security, and grows always more abstract. The alternative truth embodied in and performed by Moses, Elijah, Elisha, and

Jesus is *bottom-up*. It operates among and on behalf of ordinary people and concerns bodily possibility and bodily social transformation. The weight of scriptural testimony is to insist that top-down truth will never be effectively transformative and cannot be. Transformative power is released only from below. To be sure, it may happily evoke top-down action of a salutary kind, but such top-down action remains transformative only as long as it is in significant contact with bottom-up bodily reality. When that contact with bodily reality is lost or disregarded, top-down authority floats toward abstraction.

In the modern world, top down authority results from the Enlightenment reasoning of Descartes and Bacon, and yields a certain kind of certitude that is not impinged upon by the whims of human reality. This kind of reasoning is readily utilized by concentrations of great wealth and power:

- Thus nation states can together commit great violence, without blinking at the "necessary" devastation. Thus witness Hiroshima or Dresden.
- Thus banks can readily mandate foreclosure on marginal housing for unpaid rent, without blinking at the desperation of resourceless people.
- Thus universities can easily admit legacy students or children of major donors, without blinking at the disregard of resourceless students who are well qualified but who do not "qualify."

Such abstract reasoning is everywhere among us as it functions consistently as an ally of great wealth and power. While such "truth" is no respecter of persons, it is indeed often a respecter of wealth. It is not difficult to conclude that governments, banks, universities, and the media are allied in their great attentiveness to truth from above that tends to be abstract, quantifiable, drawn to a certain kind of rationality, and generated by and for the entitled.

We may take a deep breath to recognize that it is *quotidian truth from below* that is entrusted to the church. It is the peculiar mandate of the church to be in solidarity with those left behind and those left out. This is truth with *a creaturely face* that is marked by disjunction, disruption, and need, "without form or comeliness." The church is an heir to the claims of Jesus. He was asked by John the Baptist if he was the Messiah. John, via the tradition, no doubt had in mind pedigree, ancient memory, and legitimate norms for any messianic claim. Jesus' response to John's query, however, is quite otherwise:

> The blind receive their sight, the lame walk, the lepers are cleansed, the deaf hear, the dead are raised, the poor have good news brought to them (Luke 7:22).

That is all! This is an inventory of those who remain unqualified, without claim or resource.

Blind, lame, lepers, dead, poor!

They are the peculiar province of Jesus' preoccupation. Consequently they are the peculiar charge to the church. To be sure, sometimes the church is seduced. We in the church, as much as anyone, like beauty, property, and grandeur. We stage impressive liturgical dramas. We build exotic edifices. All of that, however, is insistently assessed by the norm of real people in their bodily reality. When the church is seduced away from its proper truth, it is characteristically called back with a reminder that our leader "suffered under Pontius Pilate, died, and was buried."

It is no wonder that the Roman governor expressed his confusion and bewilderment as Jesus stood before him.

Pilate asked him, "What is truth?" (John 18:38)

He saw before him Jesus in his acute vulnerability. And he had all around him the trappings of Roman imperial power. Present before him that day were indeed "two kinds of truth" that he could not compute or sort out. But he had an inkling. He knows that imperial power could not and did not impact Jesus. In the end he opted, as he inevitably would, for the power to which he was inured. He subsumed the truth of Jesus to the truth of the empire. He acquitted him:

> Pilate then called together the chief priests, the leaders, and the people, and said to them, "You brought me this man as one who was perverting the people; and here I have examined him in your presence and have not found this man guilty of any of your charges against him. Neither has Herod, for he sent him back to us. Indeed, he has done nothing to deserve death. I will therefore have him flogged and release him" (Luke 23:13-15).

But finally power from the people was too compelling, and Pilate gave in.

Israel was always standing before the either/or of Mt. Carmel:

> How long will you go limping with two different opinions? If the Lord is God, follow him; but if Baal, then follow him
> (I Kings 18:21).

And so the church is likewise always standing before the same either/or. We have no doubt where our true purpose and mandate rest. That is why we are privileged, regularly, to re-embrace our commitment to truth from below, one neighbor at a time. Absent truth from below we can "love God" as a generic mandate. Truth from below, by contrast, knows that the only love of God that has any substance is love of God enacted as love of neighbor. We know this through the prism of this counter-tradition of covenant that is always one neighbor at a time, every neighbor a carrier of that truth that no force from above can override or cancel out. We have many liturgical prompts through which we may keep our energy and attention focused on this truth entrusted to us.

CHAPTER SIX

The Father God Who Is No God-Father

In the course of a family household, there are characteristically two most demanding, most rewarding relationships: the relationship of *marital partners* and the relationship of *parent and child*. (A third derivative demanding and rewarding relationship is that between *siblings*.) In Fences, a play by August Wilson, Tory is the main character. He is a steady, reliable Black garbage collector who does his work every day, loves his family, and seeks out chances for small gains. In the play, Troy has a tangle with both of these primary relationships.

On the one hand, he is deeply in love with and attentive to Rose, his steadfast second wife. In the course of the play, however, Troy runs aground in his relationship with Rose by engaging in a sexual relationship outside his marriage. In that relationship, moreover, Troy produces a child who eventually must be cared for by Rose.

On the other hand, Troy has two sons. His older son, Lyons, comes and goes, borrows money from his father and pays it back. Troy eventually is stern with Lyons and says that he will no longer loan him more money. My interest, however, is in Troy's relationship with his second son, Cory. Cory is a much younger son who is ambitious to be an athlete, but is quite unwilling to do any of the work chores that Troy expects of him. Troy invites Cory to reflect on why Troy has so reliably cared for him and given him all he has needed in his growing-up years.

Troy and Cory discuss the fact that Troy has been an unfailingly good provider for Cory. Cory speculates about Troy's motivation for such care and provision:

'Cause you like me?

In response Troy delivers a reflection about his duty as a father:

> It's my job. It's my responsibility! You understand that? A man got to take care of his family. You live in my house…sleep you behind on my bedclothes…fill you belly with my food…cause you my son. You my flesh and blood. Not 'cause I like you! Cause it's my duty to take care of you. I owe a responsibility to you! Let's get this straight right here…before it go along any further…I ain't got to like you. Mr. Rand don't give me my money come payday cause he likes me. He gives me cause he owe me. I done give you everything I had to give you. I gave you your life! Me and your mama worked that out between us. And liking your black ass wasn't part of the bargain. Don't you try and go through life worrying about if somebody like you or not. You best be making sure they doing right by you. You understand what I'm saying, boy? (p. 38)

When he finishes, Troy dismisses Cory to go on down to work. Cory, determined to play football, will not go to work. He has been brought to understand, nonetheless, what it means to have a reliable father and what it means to be on the receiving end of such fatherly attentiveness.

Later on the father and son clash again. In his teenage impudence, Cory mocks his father:

> You ain't got to worry about what I got.

In response Troy delivers his harsh dismissal of his son:

> You right! You one hundred percent right! I done spent the last seventeen years worrying about what you got. Now it's your

turn, see? I'll tell you what to do. You grown…we done established that. You a man. Now, let's see you act like one. Turn your behind around and walk out this yard. And when you get out there in the alley…you can forget about this house. See? Cause this is my house. You go on and be a man and get your own house. You can forget about this. 'Cause this is mine. You go on and get yours cause I'm through with doing for you (p. 86).

In a fit of unreality, Cory answers his father defiantly:

You talking about what you did for me…what'd you ever give me?

Troy is quick in response:

Them feet and bones! That pumping heart, nigger! I give you more than anybody else is ever gonna give you.

Cory's feeble face-saving is pitiful:

You ain't never gave me nothing! You ain't never done nothing but hold me back.

Thus the sad dance of father and son who are so deeply tied together, both unable to manage the strain of growing up and the liminal stage of quasi-independence.

Wilson's rendering of father and son inescapably got me thinking about the way in which the Bible utilizes the imagery of "father" in its articulation of God. This scriptural material is rich and dense, and moves into depths well below any simplistic piety. Here I will treat only a few aspects of the rich imagery.

Quite without any warning or expectation, the metaphor emerges on the lips of YHWH in the Exodus narrative:

> Thus says the Lord: Israel is my firstborn son. I said to you,
> "Let my son go that he may worship me." (Exodus 4:22-23)

YHWH takes Israel as "firstborn son" with all the privileges and expectations of that role. The father, moreover, wills that his firstborn son, yet in slavery, should be free to "worship me." The imagery is thick; sonship is clearly linked to both emancipation and allegiance to YHWH as father. The gift of *emancipation* and the reality of *allegiance* to YHWH cannot be separated. Pharaoh's refusal of YHWH's request is promptly a warrant for the slaughter of Pharaoh's firstborn son and his heir apparent (v. 23). These verses set in motion the rich imagery of the metaphor for what follows in the text.

The eruptive formulation of father and son in Exodus 4:22-23 evokes the prophetic allusion in Hosea 11:1-9. Here as well, Israel is "my son" called out of Egypt. This text in Hosea is one of the most important texts for our study; it participates fully in the drama of fatherhood and sonship. In vv. 1-4 YHWH reminisces about the wondrous time early on when son Israel was learning to walk and needing to be fed. The words portray affectionate intimacy concerning a time of innocent dependence.

But then in vv. 5-7, the beloved baby son has grown in a way that evokes the father's rage. We are not told why the father's rage, except that son "was bent on turning from me." Perhaps the words mark the surging independence of adolescence and the will to be free from fatherly restraints, thus a parallel to Cory. In any case the father is not only disappointed, but is furious and willing to leave the son to the sorry future he has unwittingly chosen in his recalcitrant autonomy. The shift from *affection* in vv. 1-4 to *fury* in 5-7 is not hard to believe, when we reflect on the crisis evoked by the son's chosen autonomy.

But then the father pauses (vv. 8-9). The father reflects on how it is with his son. The father does an emotional U-turn from verses 5-7. The four rhetorical questions of verse 8 imagine that the upheaval in the father ("heart recoils") is not unlike the *quaking* of Sodom and Gomorrah (that is, Admah and Zeboiim; see Genesis 19:25). The same verb (*hpk*; "overthrow, recoil") occurs in both texts. The self-critical questions lead to fresh self-awareness and resolve by the father. The outcome of this reflection by the father is that the father experiences a wave of compassion for his wayward son. The resolve of verse 9 is that the father retreats from the rage of verses 5-7 (albeit a fully merited rage), remembers what he intends to be as the father God who will not act like a human father who too easily ends in rage. YHWH will not be like Troy! We may conclude that Hosea 11:1-9 enunciates a decisive moment in the self-understanding of YHWH as father. His son's waywardness had pushed the father to destructive rage; this reflective moment, however, permitted the father to make a different kind of response.

Eventually we arrive at the dread post-exilic days when Israel is bereft of possibility. A segment of Israel alienated from the tradition can pray as it acknowledges its dire circumstance and its desperate need:

> For you are our father,
> though Abraham does not know us
> and Israel does not acknowledge us;
> You, O Lord, are our father,
> our Redeemer from of old is your name (Isaiah 63:16).

The reference to "redeemer" surely recalls the Exodus emancipation. That is who YHWH is and how YHWH has acted as delivering father. The company that speaks here looks back even behind the tradition of Abraham. Behind and before Abraham, there is father-YHWH. This is "our redeemer" "from of old," that is, at least since the Exodus. Israel has no alternative but to trust finally in the fatherliness of YHWH who is a sure protector and rescuer. This is the plea of those who must now rely on the goodness of the father. This address in 63:16 leads to the desperate petition of 64:8-9. In a mix of images (father, potter) Israel understands that its life is completely given by and dependent upon YHWH. That dependence and reliance become the ground for the petition in verse 64:9 with three imperative verbs:

> Yet, O Lord, you are our Father;
> we are the clay, and you are our potter;
> we are all the work of your hand.
> *Do not be exceedingly angry*, O Lord,
> and *do not remember* iniquity forever.
> Now *consider*, we are all your people (64:8-9).

What follows in verses 10-11 make the situation as urgent and grim as could possibly be for the creator God. The petition ends with two desperate questions:

> After all this,
> will you restrain yourself, O Lord?
> Will you keep silence, and punish us so severely? (64:12)

In its plea Israel finds it impossible to imagine that in this circumstance YHWH will be restrained or silent. Everything for Israel's wellbeing and future depends upon the father-potter and the willingness of the father to intervene. But then, that has been so since the ancient days of the Exodus. In its good times son-Israel can imagine its autonomy and self-sufficiency, not unlike Cory. In desperate times Israel knows better, something Cory still has to learn in his future.

The God
>who called Israel into being in Egypt,
>who moved from anger to compassion in Hosea, and
>who is addressed in urgent petition in Isaiah,

is the God who reemerges in the parable of Jesus. The triad of parables (sheep, coin, son) in Luke 15 is in response to the dismissive mockery of the Pharisees and scribes. The Pharisees and scribes lived in a closed totalism of religious certitude. They saw that Jesus' work refused to remain in their cozy totalism, because he welcomed and ate with those they had dismissed as ineligible. Each of these parables concerns a rejected member of a collective, a lost sheep, a lost coin, and a lost son.

The father inescapably had two sons, not unlike Troy. One of Troy's sons had moved on, managing his independence in fragile ways. One of the sons in the family of Luke 15 had not moved on, but he had accepted familial responsibility and fully understood his duties and his prospects. The other son in the parable is not unlike Cory. He imagined a life of self-indulgent ease and success. We are not told how it worked out for Cory. It did not work out for the son in the parable, as we get to see him to the end. We can imagine that Cory, sometime later, had to come back home in need, but we do not know how Troy might have responded to such a return. There is some reason to expect that Troy might have softened to his wayward son in need. But we do know about this other father, the one featured in the parable.

This father in the parable, the one who had designated his son in Egypt and had fought through to compassion, was on the lookout for his son. He expected him back in his need. He was prepared to receive him with a generous welcome:

> But while he was still far off, his father saw him and was filled with compassion; he ran and put his arms around him and kissed him (Luke 15:20).

The son had no grounds for such a reception and was prepared to grovel before his father. But the father interrupted the son's prepared speech of groveling. The father's interruption of the son led to a gracious, celebrative homecoming with no questions asked, no explanations required, and no scores to be settled:

> This son of mine was dead and is alive again; he was lost and is found (v. 24)!

And just so that everyone, including the older son, could understand, the father reiterates the new beginning with his wayward son:

> This brother of yours was dead and has come to life; he was lost and has been found (Luke 15:32).

Imagine! It is to this father, the one to whom Moses, Hosea, Isaiah, and Jesus bear witness, that we dare to pray:

> Our father!
> Our father (who is in heaven), that is, not a father defined by the quid *pro quo calculus* of Pharaoh.

It is to this father that we dare to pray:

> from this father we ask *forgiveness*;
> from this father we hope for *daily bread* that we cannot produce ourselves;
> from this father we anticipate *protection from evil*.

We pray in such a way to this father, even as we acknowledge him to be potter as we are clay, the creator to whom belongs all the governance of the kingdom, all the power of creation, all the glory of our grateful world.

> To this father belong all *the kingdom, the power, and the glory!*

This God is no pushover. This God is no good buddy suburban dad, but the one who presides over our life with dignity and gravitas. It turns out that both sons must come to terms with a household governed by the gracious will of the father. Troy, of course, does not reason that far. Nor do any of our earthly fathers! It is for that reason that after we know the graciousness of our earthly fathers, we are still left in awe before the father-God who does "so much more!" (Matthew 7:9-11, Luke 11:11-13). This long-term sketch of God as father delivers to us a reliable world governed by generous compassion. It only requires us to "come to ourselves" and come home (Luke 15:17), away from any other life that we may have "squandered" (Luke 15:13). We may have squandered it in self-indulgence. Or we may have squandered it in fear and parsimony. Either way, we squander and then are stunned by this contrasting welcome of generous compassion. We may learn a great deal from the life-story of Troy. There is much more to be said beyond Troy's vexed narrative. It is no wonder that the final lines of Wilson's play must focus on the word and action of Gabriel.

> Troy, you ready? You ready, Troy. I'm gonna tell St. Peter to open the gates. You get ready now. (Gabriel blows and sings and dances.) That's the way to go! (pp. 100-101)

Wilson takes Troy out of his normal habitat into a zone of unimaginable wellbeing. That is what the father does for the son in the parable. It is not escapism, but a chance for an alternative life. The invitation of Gabriel to Troy sounds not unlike an arrival "with Abraham" (Luke 16:22).

Now a *challenge*: This rendition of God as father is cast in generous terms, but nonetheless in patriarchal imagery. This sketch, I suggest, invites us in our present circumstance to construct a parallel rendition of *the mother God* who "comforts" (Isaiah 65:13), and who summons to adulthood. It is my hope that some reader will take on this task and so bring to fresh fruition the imagining of scripture.

CHAPTER SEVEN

The Empowering, Illuminating Word From Elsewhere

> Your word is a lamp to my feet
> and a light to my path (Psalm 119:105).

A few Sundays ago our well-spoken pastor, Joan, recited this biblical verse as the salutation at the outset of her sermon. She did not comment further on the verse, but proceeded in a compelling way to articulate the "path/way" of the gospel to which the verse refers.

I have long had a special personal attachment to this verse. In my growing up context of evangelical pietism in the "E and R" tradition, it was the custom that the pastor assigned to each thirteen-year-old confirmand a "confirmation verse." That verse was taken to be a marker of faith for the confirmand, and was often recalled and reiterated many years later at the funeral of the deceased confirmand. In my case, my pastor (also my father) assigned this as my confirmation verse. Nothing was made of it at the time, but for a long time now in retrospect I have pondered my father's choice of the verse for me, given that I have spent my adult life engaged with and expositing the "word" of the biblical text. As a consequence I have taken his assignment of this verse to me as a thirteen-year-old as a providential act in anticipation of the adult life and work that have long occupied me.

The verse occurs in the longest of the Psalms, Psalm 119. That long Psalm is shaped as the most artful and well-developed acrostic poem in scripture. An "acrostic" is a poetic articulation that proceeds through the alphabet with each successive line beginning with the next letter from A to Z, that is in Hebrew, from *'aleph* to *taw*. We have other acrostic poems in the Old Testament that run the course of the alphabet as a way of completeness. (See Psalms 25, 34, 37, 111, 145, and Proverbs 31:10-31, Lamentations 1-4.) The scholar who has most intently and vigorously studied the acrostic pattern is J. P. Fokkelman, *Major Poems of the Hebrew Bible: At the Interface of Prosody and Structural Analysis*, 2000). In each of these texts the alphabetic sequence is traced, though some of the poetry does not complete the task. Psalm 119, however, is exceptional. In all the other cases of acrostic each letter of the Hebrew alphabet occurs once in sequence. In Psalm 119, by contrast, each letter gets eight successive lines. Thus with twenty-two letters in the alphabet, and each letter reiterated eight times, we get a sum of 176 verses. It is for that reason that the Psalm is so long. Our verse 105 occurs as the first of eight verses that start with *nun* (n) (vv. 105-112). The first word in verse 105, the first of eight lines with *nun*, is "*ner*" (lamp). Unfortunately none of this is evident in English translation.

One can readily see in the Psalm a cluster of terms that are variously repeated and reiterated:

> Commandment, decree, judgment, law (Torah), ordinance, precept, statute, word.

We may take all of these several terms as rough synonyms, all of which refer to the written Torah. The written Torah (never without thick interpretation) is a "lamp" and a "light." It serves to illumine the path/way in which covenanted Israel is to walk. We may notice the same parallelism in Jeremiah 6:16:

> Thus says the Lord:
> Stand at the crossroads, and look,
> and ask for the ancient *paths*,
> where the good *way* lies; and walk in it,
> and find rest for your souls (Jeremiah 6:16).

The ancient path/way is surely the way of Torah that Jeremiah commended in chapter 11. In this verse the prophet laments that Israel has chosen not to walk in that path/way. Concerning the parallelism, remarkably in Proverbs 8:20, personified wisdom affirms the substance of the path/way commended in covenant:

> I (wisdom) walk in the *way* of righteousness,
> and the *paths* of justice.

Thus the path/way of Torah is the *righteousness and justice* that enact love of God and love of neighbor. While wisdom commends that way/path, the prophet sees that Israel refuses to walk in it. Thus in considering the path/way of covenanted Israel, we are able to see the deep insistence and radicality of our verse that is so innocent-looking. The path/way of Israel, enunciated in the Torah of Sinai, is an alternative path/way, alternative to the predation of Pharaoh, alternative to the extravagance of Solomon, and alternative to the brutality of Babylon. It is plausible, moreover, that this cluster of terms in the Psalm refers more explicitly to the Book of Deuteronomy and to the trajectory of Torah interpretation that ensues from and is advocated by the Book of Deuteronomy. Thus Gerhard von Rad, *Studies in Deuteronomy* (p. 16), could see that Deuteronomy was "preached law," so that the preaching (interpretive proclamation) of the Torah of Deuteronomy became the engine of Judaism as reflected in the leadership of Ezra and in the sermonic content of the Books of Chronicles.

This same trajectory of an alternative path/way comes to clear expression in the teaching of Jesus:

> Enter through the narrow gate; for the gate is wide and the road is easy that leads to destruction, and there are many who take it. For the gate is narrow and the road is hard that leads to life, and there are few who find it (Matthew 7:13-14; see Luke 13:24).

In the horizon of Jesus, this path/way consisted of discipleship that required leaving all else to "follow." This characterization of the alternative community around Jesus as "followers of the way" (Acts 9:2, 24:14) indicates the requirements that we know as "love of God" and "love of neighbor." This narrow, hard way is an alternative to the broad, easy way of the world marked by self-sufficiency and self-securing. Discipleship to Jesus is indeed an articulation of covenantal obedience to the alternative of Torah. The Torah provides guidance and illumination for how to live this alternative life in the world.

Alternatively, Karl Barth parses the matter differently. He takes "the word" to be the decisive articulation of God. It is this *logos* (logic that pervades creation) that is the force of the creator who "calls the world into being." It is, moreover, this same "word" that is bodily present in the person of Jesus "full of grace and truth." But then boldly Barth goes further to aver that the word that creates and the word that is enfleshed in Jesus is the word as the *written witness* of scripture that comes to powerful performance in the *word as sermon*. This breathtaking force of the word in these several modes is contrasted to a world "formless and void" that is without the ordering, life-giving power of the word. Such a world devoid of the word is a world unto death.

All of this was readily on the table when our pastor moved

easily from the initial salutation to her sermon on John 6:3-13 and the wonder of the loaves multiplied in order to feed a hungry crowd. She nicely finessed every "explanation" for the delivery of bread, as the four gospels, each in turn, refuses to "explain" this spectacular wonder. The text is a story, not an argument. It is a specific narrative, not a logical syllogism. The wonder of the narrative is the affirmation that in the fleshly word of Jesus' own person the capacity of the creator God for abundance is readily available. Our pastor traced through two other narratives of abundant bread in the manna story of Exodus 16 and the wonder of bread wrought through Elisha (II Kings 4:42-44). Her proclamation concerned the radical claim that the world governed by the creator God teems with life-giving abundance, an abundance that is quite unlike and contrasted with the world around us that is dominated by fear, greed, and violence, and thus by scarcity.

The sermon concerned the demanding either/or of scarcity-abundance. There is no doubt that our present world is powerfully dominated by an ideology of scarcity. It is this ideology that propels tax policy, readiness for war, and our greedy arguments for the exclusion and disregard of the poor, the vulnerable, and the "undeserving." The claim of the sermon—the claim of the Torah, the claim of the gospel—is that we may walk in the light that illumines a different path of glad obedience in the world. (On the parallel claims in Judaism and Christianity, see James A. Sanders, "Torah and Christ," *Interpretation 29* (1975).) In ancient Israel that walk is the path/way of *covenant*. In the story of Jesus, it is the glad walk of *discipleship*. Taken either way, it is a summons to live differently, to live with the truth of God's abundance in a way that resists and refuses the fear of scarcity so evident in our society. It follows that on that path/way we may be free of fear and of greed and, consequently, free of every temptation to violence.

I had two thoughts as I reflected on my confirmation verse and the sermon that followed it a few Sundays ago. First, I understood afresh the South African hymn, *Siyahamba*:

> We are marching in the light,
> We are marching in the light of God,
> We are marching in the light of God,
> We are marching, marching,
> We are marching…

That "march" about which Blacks sing in South Africa is a march of faith that resists, rejects, and refuses the social reality of Apartheid and exclusiveness. That has been a hard, risky march in South Africa, just as it is always a hard, demanding alternative to the easier path of the status quo.

Second, as we gathered to hear our pastor line out the alternative path/way of abundance and generosity, it dawned on me afresh that serious discipleship requires that we be *at the meeting of the faithful* regularly, always again, in order to participate in the performance of the alternative path/way. The reason we must always be at the meeting of the faithful is that we are regularly and forcefully bombarded by the regent path/way of scarcity. Indeed, our pastor began her sermon by pointing out how the narrative of scarcity was everywhere pervasive including in the interminable TV ads. It is the work of "the meeting" to counter that bombardment, and to remind us of our alternative path/way. The utterance of the word does indeed guide our path/way. Without that word uttered and heard we may, much too readily, stray to the wide, easy path of scarcity that leads to "destruction"! (Matthew 7:13)

CHAPTER EIGHT

The Good Shepherd and the Bad Ones

Without any great intentionality I have been reading about the cruel bite that neoliberal politics puts on vulnerable poor people. In case you might want to see some of that literature, my reading has included:

> Juan Gonzalez, *Harvest of Empire: A History of Latinos in America* (New York: Viking Press, 2000)

> Frances Fox Piven and Richard A. Cloward, *Regulating the Poor: The Public Functions of Welfare* (New York: Vintage, 1993)

> Joe Soss, Richard C. Fording, and Sanford F. Schram, *Disciplining the Poor: Neoliberal Paternalism and the Persistent Power of Race* (Chicago: University of Chicago Press, 2011)

> Loïc Wanquant, *Punishing the Poor: The Neoliberal Government of Social Insecurity* (Durham: Duke University Press, 2009)

The gist of the argument is that in the 1990s, under the leadership of President Clinton and Governor Jeb Bush in Florida, neoliberal politics surged, imposing new and rigorous demands on the vulnerable poor. The outcome was an attempt to reduce the working poor to a reliable and essential cog in the production machinery that generated even greater wealth for those at the top of society. The human face of the poor disappeared in this redirection to a workforce on the cheap, without influence or voice.

I gained access to this heavy issue through the commentary of Soss, Fording and Schram concerning the changing role of a case manager. Heretofore a case manager might be concerned for the general welfare of a poor client. Now, however, the single duty of a case manager is to assure work predictability and reliability. A case manager attests:

> [Welfare in Florida] is no longer a social service; it is a business. I find it to be the difference between herding cattle and herding sheep. A cattle herder is just running people through, not taking time to look after them.

The authors comment:

> Following this metaphor, we may say that sanctions provide a "prod" for case managers who must find a way to "herd their cattle." In explaining this dynamic, one case manager also touched on how sanctions can promote the paternalistic goal of instilling self-discipline (240).

Later on, the metaphor is extended:

> "A cattle herder is just running people through, not taking time to look after them. A shepherd takes care of the sheep, tends after them, cares for them. It is not my nature to herd cattle and now I have to learn to do that." A welfare client interviewed by Soss (2000) reached for the same metaphor, among other illuminating comparisons, to convey her feelings of subordination and frustration: "It's like you're in a cattle prod. It's like you're in a big mill. I felt like a number, or like I was in a prison system. Like I said, it feels like you're in a cattle prod. They're the cowboys and you're a cow. [T]hese people are like 'just be quiet and follow your line.'" (285)

The contrast between "herding cattle" and "caring for sheep" helped me to see something of what is at stake.

Beyond that, the image of sheep-shepherd helped me to make a link to biblical imagery. I turned first of all to Ezekiel 34, perhaps the most important biblical text concerning governing responsibility. (It is to be noted that as long ago as Hammurabi in Old Babylon, "shepherd" has been a figure for "king," suggesting a regal responsibility for the royal subjects who are as vulnerable as sheep.) In the prophetic oracle Ezekiel begins with a condemnation of "the shepherds" who have been negligent in their duty and have only engaged in self-serving indulgence:

> Mortal, prophesy against the shepherds of Israel…Thus says the Lord God: Ah, you shepherds of Israel who have been feeding yourselves! Should not shepherds feed the sheep? You eat the fat, you clothe yourselves with the wool, you slaughter the fatlings; but you do not feed the sheep. You have not strengthened the weak, you have not healed the sick, you have not bound up the injured, you have not brought back the strayed, you have not sought the lost, but with force and harshness you have ruled them. So they were scattered, because there was no shepherd; and scattered, they became food for all the wild animals. My sheep were scattered, they wandered over all the mountains and on every high hill; my sheep were scattered over all the face of the earth, with no one to search or seek for them (Ezekiel 34:2-6).

The critique concerns the long run of failed Davidic kings in Jerusalem. Of these kings we may mention two in particular:

Concerning Manasseh:

> Moreover Manasseh shed very much innocent blood, until he had filled Jerusalem from one end to another, besides the sin that he caused Judah to sin so that they did what was evil in the sight of the Lord (II Kings 21:16).

Concerning Jehoiakim:

> Woe to him who builds his house by unrighteousness,
> and his upper rooms by injustice;
> who makes his neighbors work for nothing,
> and does not give them their wages (Jeremiah 22:13).

The charge is that such self-serving neglect on the part of the king leads to big trouble for "the flock," in this case, exile and displacement. As a consequence, Ezekiel can have God declare:

> I am against the shepherds; and I will demand my sheep at their hand, and put a stop to their feeding the sheep; no longer shall the shepherds feed themselves. I will rescue my sheep from their mouths, so that they may not be food for them (Ezekiel 34:10).

It is the recurring practice of "bad shepherds" to exploit the sheep for their own advantage. The sheep are exposed, vulnerable, and helpless. And God is mightily provoked.

We might imagine a sheep with some poetic imagination reciting a (newly discovered) Psalm concerning "the bad shepherd":

> Mammon is my shepherd; I lack everything.
> Mammon leads me into dangerous places;
>   he leads me to run great risks.

> He depletes my *nephesh*.
> He leads me into dangerous sweatshops for his own gain.
> Even though I must climb high hills to see Mammon and all
> his commodities,
> I am scared to death,
> for I never get free of him.
> His rod and staff harshly discipline me.
> They leave me vexed and frightened.
> The table on offer is cheap, bad-tasting food,
> I must eat on the run.
> My head is exposed to the dangers of big cranes and bulldozers;
> my cup runs dry with no time to drink.
> Surely greed and cruelty will chase me down,
> 'til I die in the midst of sweat and exhaustion.

It is not hard to see that the *intense regulation of neoliberal ideology* is an echo of the *old predatory kings* who cared not at all for their subjects.

The good news of Ezekiel, however, concerns the intervention of YHWH into every governance of the failed shepherd kings:

> I myself will search for my sheep, and will seek them out. As shepherds seek out their flocks when they are among their scattered sheep, so I will seek out my sheep. I will rescue them from all the places to which they have been scattered on a day of clouds and thick darkness. I will bring them out from the peoples and gather them from the countries, and will bring them into their own land; and I will feed them on the mountains of Israel, by the watercourses, and in all the inhabited parts of the land. I will feed them with good pasture, and the mountain heights of Israel shall be their pasture; there they shall lie down in good grazing land, and they shall feed on rich pasture on the mountains of Israel. I myself will be the shepherd of my sheep,

and I will make them lie down, says the Lord God. I will seek the lost, and I will bring back the strayed, and I will bind up the injured, and I will strengthen the weak, but the fat and the strong I will destroy. I will feed them with justice (Ezekiel 34:11-16).

The failed shepherd-kings will be displaced. YHWH will undertake direct rule to prevent the violent greed of the kings. God is able to see and remove the negligent shepherds who exploit the lean sheep.

Now we get a shifted metaphor that concerns the aggression of *fat sheep* against the *lean sheep*:

> I myself will judge between the fat sheep and the lean sheep. Because you have pushed with flank and shoulder, and butted at all the weak animals with your horns until you scattered them far and wide, I will save my flock, and they shall no longer be ravaged; and I will judge between sheep and sheep (Ezekiel 34:20-22).

There is no exact cognate in our economic situation to the intervention of God. We may, however, imagine that the government might intervene on behalf of the vulnerable who are exposed to aggressive exploitation. Except, of course, the neoliberal ideology that justifies the exploitation that has largely come to dominate government, so that it is quite unlikely that such an intervention may occur.

Only at the end of this prophetic oracle do we get mention of human agency:

> I will set up over them one shepherd, my servant David, and he shall feed them; he shall feed them and be their shepherd. And I, the Lord, will be their God, and my servant David shall be prince among them; I, the Lord, have spoken (Ezekiel 34:23-24).

The prophet can anticipate a coming Davidic king who will do the work of the good shepherd. This coming David will not be a king," but only "a prince among" who is accountable to the shepherd king, God. Thus Ezekiel can anticipate that the exploitative rule of the bad shepherds will come to an end. It is this anticipation that leads to the expectation that in time to come a king-Messiah will govern in justice, mercy, and equity.

It is my thought that we in the church will do well to place the social analysis of Ezekiel 34 front and center in our pondering of our new socioeconomic reality. The vision of the prophet revolves around the conviction that the purpose of government is *the protection and wellbeing of the vulnerable*, exactly a contradiction to the neoliberal practice that is programmatically *exploitative of the vulnerable*. The literature I have mentioned above variously uses terms like "regulating, disciplining, and punishing" as harsh acts against the poor in order to force the poor into submission as cheap labor. Such words are contradicted by those of the good shepherd: "seek out, rescue, gather, and feed." The latter words indicate the work to be done to rescue the vulnerable from the bad shepherds.

There is no doubt that the "shepherd-sheep" imagery of Ezekiel with the expectation of a "new David" is reflected in the presentation of Jesus in the gospel narrative. Specifically, we may reference the imagery of John 10:1-16. In this poetic rendering of Jesus, we do not get "bad shepherds," but we get "thieves and bandits" (vv. 1, 8), a "stranger" (v. 8), and a "hired hand" (vv. 12-13). All of these are contrasted to the "good shepherd" because they do not know or care for the sheep; the sheep, moreover, do not know them or trust them. Thus the "thieves and bandits" only come to "steal and kill and destroy" (v. 10). The sheep run from the stranger (v. 5). And the hired hand deserts the sheep in a time of crisis (v. 12). If we consider these several negations together, we have a good representation of the regard neoliberal ideology has for the vulnerable poor. That ideology does not know them; they seek out the poor to steal, kill, or destroy for the sake of greater wealth. They readily abandon the sheep in a crisis, i.e., as soon as their profit fades. The image is of *vulnerable sheep* and *alien agents in the sheepfold* who do not care at all for the sheep.

By contrast, it is Jesus who follows in the prophetic train of wise, caring attentiveness whose life is given over to the wellbeing of his vulnerable subjects. It is the extreme expression of care for the sheep that the shepherd will place himself in danger in order to protect the sheep. In this phrase "lay down his life" (v. 17), we may stay within the imagery and imagine a shepherd fending off a wolf or a lion for the sake of keeping the sheep safe. The radical self-giving for the wellbeing of the other is at the heart of a gospel ethic, a profound contradiction to the greedy economy that treats the poor as readily expendable.

It is an obvious truism that the church is to persist in the work of Jesus. Thus we may imagine that as the "good shepherd" gives his life for the sheep, so is the church in its work of such self-giving for the poor and vulnerable. In the Fourth Gospel the imagery moves readily from the *claim for Christ* in chapter 10 to *the mandate for the church* in chapter 21. In that final exchange between Jesus and his lead disciple, Peter is told three times how to express his love toward the Lord Jesus:

> Feed my lambs (v. 15);
> Tend my sheep (v. 16);
> Feed my sheep (v. 17).

The allusion to the execution of Peter in verses 18-19 voices the extreme mandate of the Gospel to lay down life for the vulnerable.

> The sequence is from *royal ideology* (king as shepherd), to
> *prophetic condemnation* and *anticipation*, to
> the *rendering of Jesus as Good Shepherd*, to
> the *church as sheep-tenders*.

This sequence provides a rich theme for our reflection on the economy and on governance. This trajectory on the one hand clearly voices the mandate to the church. On the other hand, the trajectory voices a thematic for our thought about governance, the shape of government policy, and the deployment of public resources. For a church that continues to be excessively preoccupied with personal salvation and next-world prospects, this thematic is an urgent invitation. The matter is made even more urgent by the fact that in our economy there are very few witnesses left who can provide a critical stance against neoliberal greed and violence. It is not enough that the vulnerable poor can participate in the economy by work that earns a livelihood. What is essential is that the vulnerable poor be given a voice in the public domain. Such voice, moreover, can only be sustained along with becoming property owners. Thus the work of government is the sustenance of such inclusive economic empowerment. We have work to do in the church that is nothing less than the recovery of the primary accents of our treasured tradition.

CHAPTER NINE

The Dispossessing Power of Violent Greed

In the summer of 1961, just before I began teaching at Eden Seminary, my then wife Mary and I led an ecumenical work camp. It was under the auspices of the National Council of Churches and was based near Rocky Mount, NC. Our home base was Franklinton Center, a congregational conference center presided over by the intrepid Dr. Judson King. The conference center was said to be the only place in North Carolina at the time where interracial meetings could be held. We were about fifteen persons, including folk from Jamaica, Lebanon, and India. Our daily work for eight weeks was to paint barns for small-acreage African American tobacco farmers. We painted with white creosote, not the most amenable concoction in hot weather!

The summer of 1961 in North Carolina, as in many places, was a time of acute racial tension. It was at the peak of Freedom Rides and Sit-ins. Judson King joked with us that the only safe way for us whites to travel with him as an African American was to have him pose as our chauffeur. We pretty much stayed at our work and at our common life as a community, and did not interact as much with the farm families as we might have done. We had only one external excursion when, one day, we all drove two hundred miles to get to an integrated sea coast where we could swim together. In retrospect I understood very little about the demanding dynamics of the socio-economics of those farmers beyond the obvious reality of racial tension and the ominous sense that violence could not be very far away.

As a result I was not well prepared for the book I am currently reading, *Dispossession: Discrimination against African American Farmers in the Age of Civil Rights*, by Pete Daniel (2013). Daniel provides excruciating chapter and verse concerning the systemic way in which small-acreage Black farmers were squeezed into debt and eventually forced to give up their acreage of farm land. The pivot point of such systemic racist dispossession was in the US Department of Agriculture. Since Franklin Roosevelt, the Department has provided generous funds to sustain farmers. But the support and money of the Department was filtered through and administered by local county Extension Agents who were able to operate without accountability according to local racist assumptions. As a result, the money of the Department was regularly assigned to White farmers while Black farmers were denied access to funding. The Department in DC mostly disregarded the local racist administrators with "feckless acquiescence" (p. 135), though some Secretaries of Agriculture, among them Earl Butts and Clifford Hardin, actively colluded in the practice, so that local offices were "being run like plantations" (p. 250).

The Department, moreover, opted for big farm operations, so that preferential treatment was given the farmers who themselves were already alert to the recent gains in research and equipment, all the same to squeeze out small farmers, both White and Black, but most especially Black farmers. Thus for example,

> In its analysis of interviews in Tuscaloosa, Greene, Sumter, Hale, and Dallas Counties in Alabama, the commission found that white cattlemen could take their bulls to Auburn for fertility testing but blacks could not. Nor did blacks share equally in the cotton acreage released each year and redistributed by the ASCS committee. White county agents worked on Cattlemen's

> Association and Farm Bureau projects, but African Americans could not belong to the Cattlemen's Association and rarely attended presentations by specialists in field crops, dairy, or livestock (45).

Daniel's study especially focuses on the early 60s (exactly the time of our work camp), just after *Brown v. Topeka* and just as the Voting Rights Act was enacted. Along with these immensely important court rulings and congressional acts, the peak of sit-ins and freedom rides made the social context of Daniel's study ripe with issues of civil rights. Thus he reports:

> After the *Brown* decision and more intensely after the Civil Rights Act of 1964, the Extension Service used its trifurcated federal-state-county identity to foil civil rights initiatives. Although it was a federal agency, its programs operated out of white land-grant universities, and because counties contributed to funding, there was also a substantial local dimension. USDA civil rights initiatives passed through these strata much like laundered money. Washington administrators announced support of civil rights, land-grant universities gave lip service but recast directives to suit their own purposes, and by the time regulations reached counties, they were unrecognizable as federal civil rights currency (34).

Daniel reviews in some detail the tribulation of James Mays and his brothers in Leesburg in Lee County, Alabama. Mays, a school teacher, secured an operating loan from FHA. But the county supervisor reviewed the decision and denied the loan. As a teacher Mays had defended a student paper that had critiqued the school:

> He was asked to resign his teaching position in June 1962. That fall, he was denied an operating loan when the FHA questioned

his ability to repay it and cited a negative character check. Mays did not appeal. He applied in October 1963 and was again denied. Unable to get credit from the FHA or from private sources in the county, he went outside the county for his loans. Two of Mays's brothers were also denied loans, presumably because of their civil rights activity. All three Mays men had canvassed with SNCC workers during the summer of 1962....The treatment of the Mays family for its civil rights work epitomized the pressure that both the USDA and the business community brought on African Americans who transgressed their assigned place in the community (39).

The aggressive role played by the USDA has continued in recent years. Now and then it has been checked by court rulings. Most important is *Strain v. Philpott* in 1971. Willie Strain was a Black advocate who eventually brought suit against Auburn University. (Philpott was the name of the president of the university.) The brave and courageous federal judge, Frank Johnson, ruled on behalf of Strain against the university. He traced out the intricate way in which the university, through like-minded administrators, had denied Strain and other Black persons equal access to money and opportunity:

> Judge Frank Johnson's decision dismembered the ACES rationale for its purportedly integrated structure. It attacked white presumptions and exposed qualifiers that perpetuated discrimination and obstructionist strategies that typified extension programs throughout the South. Johnson directed the ACES to give former African American county agents and county home-demonstration agents "first priority for consideration for all future promotions to County Extension Chairman and Associate County Extension Chairman positions respectively." If for some reason the ACES assigned a white person to such a position, it had to justify the appointment with ample documenta-

tion. Willie Strain, Thomas Agnew, and Bertha Jones "shall be given priority for consideration for all future promotions in the subject area in which they have had training and experience whether prior or subsequent to the merger of 1965"...The *Strain* decision and its implementation went a long way in erasing white privilege in Alabama's Extension Service (207-209).

A second court ruling that mattered decisively to the issue was *Timothy Pigford v. Dan Glickman* in 1999. Judge Paul. L. Friedman ruled on behalf of Black farmers (259-260). The judge took pains to notice that Black farmers were likely to lack documentation for their claims, and made allowances for their historic disadvantage. The legal redress in this matter of debt as dispossession was and is enormously important. At the same time, it is urgent to recognize that the insidious work of systemic racism continued and continues to be pervasive. That systemic effort everywhere and often does what it can to resist, reduce, and reverse the redress offered by the courts.

As I thought about the vulnerable Black farmers of our work camp experience and as I pondered Daniel's exposé, it was not a surprise that I was led, yet again, to the narrative of Naboth's vineyard (I Kings 21). The narrative is quite parallel concerning the dangerous *contest between a peasant farmer and a ruthless ruler*, or alternatively, a *contest between a covenantal notion of inherited land and a commercial understanding of land as a tradable commodity*. The narrative stands as a mighty exposé of land dispossession of the *vulnerable* by the *powerful*. In the case of Naboth, the dispossession was directly violent. In the cases cited by Daniel, the dispossession was through indebtedness that remained unresolved by government aid, even though government aid was generously available to other embedded farmers, namely, big time White farmers who had access to all the bounty that the USDA could muster for them.

In the case of US Black farmers, the important but modest redress was accomplished through the courts. In the case of Naboth, there was no such court that could stand over against the crown. Nonetheless, the Naboth narrative does end with the death of Naboth and the seizure of his land by Ahab (v. 16). The narrative continues in verses 17-29 with the appearance of Elijah. Indeed, it may be hypothesized that Elijah functions not only as the *prosecutor* but as the *Supreme Court* of the insistent governance of YHWH who, it turns out, is the ultimate arbiter of land transactions. Elijah's "ruling" is terse and prompt. The verdict is put as a question:

> Have you killed and also taken possession? (v. 19)

The sentence is swift and uncompromising:

> Thus says the Lord: In the place where dogs licked up the blood of Naboth, dogs will also lick up your blood.

The matter is elaborated so that the king will not misunderstand the future generated by his predatory action:

> Because you have sold yourself to do what is evil in the sight of the Lord, I will bring disaster on you; I will consume you, and will cut off from Ahab every male, bond or free, in Israel; and I will make your house like the house of Jeroboam son of Nebat, and like the house of Baasha son of Ahijah, because you have provoked me to anger and have caused Israel to sin. Also concerning Jezebel the Lord said, "The dogs shall eat Jezebel within the bounds of Jezreel." Anyone belonging to Ahab who dies in the city the dogs shall eat; and anyone of his who dies in the open country the birds of the air shall eat (I Kings 21:20-24).

Ahab's show of remorse in verse 27 allows for a mitigation of the sentence, but it is not retracted. The prophetic condemnation lingers and resurfaces in royal history. First, it concerns the death of Jezebel who aided and abetted the dispossession of Naboth:

> When they came back and told him, he said, "This is the word of the Lord, which he spoke by his servant Elijah the Tishbite, 'In the territory of Jezreel the dogs shall eat the flesh of Jezebel; the corpse of Jezebel shall be like dung on the field in the territory of Jezreel, so that no one can say, This is Jezebel.'" (II Kings 9:36-37)

Then it concerned the entire royal family:

> Know then that there shall fall to the earth nothing of the word of the Lord, which the Lord spoke concerning the house of Ahab; for the Lord has done what he said through his servant Elijah. So Jehu killed all who were left of the house of Ahab in Jezreel, all his leaders, close friends, and priests, until he left him no survivor (II Kings 10:10-11).

And finally the mop-up action is said to be sure and complete:

> When he came to Samaria, he killed all who were left to Ahab in Samaria, until he had wiped them out, according to the word of the Lord that he spoke to Elijah (II Kings 10:17).

Naboth is given a bloody vindication. The claim is that the ruthless dispossession of the vulnerable does not go unanswered in a world where YHWH governs. We may conclude that the court action for Black farmers cited above constituted a civic articulation of that same conviction. The matter is not as unambiguous in the contemporary case as it is in the ancient case. But the affirmation is the same; and the outcome is the same, *a defense of the vulnerable victims of predation.*

The power of predatory dispossession nonetheless continued with great effectiveness. Daniel summarizes:

> By 1910 African Americans held title to some 16 million acres of farmland, and by 1920, there were 925,000 black farms in the country. After peaking in these decades, however, the trajectory of black farmers plunged downward. In a larger sense, there was an enormous decline among all farmers at mid-century. Between 1940 and 1969, the rural transformation, fueled largely by machines and chemicals and directed by the USDA, pushed some 3.4 million farmers and their families off the land, including nearly 600,000 African Americans. From 1959 to 1969 alone, 185,000 black farmers left the land, and only 87,000 remained when Richard Nixon entered office. Farm failures were endemic, and in the 1950s, about 169,000 farm families failed annually; between 1960 and 1965, some 124,000 failed each year; and 94,000 per year failed between 1966 and 1968 (p. 6).

As we are well aware, every advance taken by the US government toward racial equality is met by fierce resistant negation. Thus in the generative years of the mid-60s in the wake of court actions and the Voting Rights legislation, the deliberate resistance of the US Department of Agriculture continued in virulent fashion.

It is hard to imagine (plus embarrassing!) how little I knew about these realities during our weeks at the work camp. Several times during our eight weeks of work we engaged the company of some of the children of the farmers. Among other things, some of the girls entertained us by singing. I recall that they sang for us the words of Engelbert Humperdinck that bore compelling witness to the divided world we occupied:

> Two different worlds
> We live in two different worlds
> For we've been told
> That a love like ours could never be
> So far apart
> They say we're so far apart
> And that we haven't the right
> To change our destiny.

In retrospect, their singing was a playful, sly acknowledgement that the world of privilege of White people in a work camp and the families of Black tobacco farmers did indeed occupy different worlds. These are, writ large, *the world of debt* and *the world of ownership*. But these girls went on to sing of Humperdinck's great hope:

> But we will show them
> As we walk together in the sun
> That our two different worlds are one.

Their singing was a gentle bit of *truth-telling* and buoyant bit of *hope-telling*, just right for those of us who had so much yet to learn.

Now it strikes me that the sore point is that I (we) did not know about this. We did not know the economic jeopardy of small-acreage Black farmers. We did not know about the long term resistance of the Department of Agriculture. We did not know about the pattern of predatory dispossession. And we did not know that we lived in a world of assets while these neighbors lived in a world of dangerous debt. We did not know, in our comfort zone so carefully protected from reality. That much has not changed. James C. Scott, *Weapons of the Weak: Everyday Forms of Peasant Resistance* (1985), has shown how the poor and vulnerable have a way to know the little controlling secrets of the ownership class, whereas the ownership class has little clue about or access to the hidden life of the poor and vulnerable.

The work of learning is an urgent responsibility, to see how and why "the other half"—the half of debt—lives and suffers and resists and fears as it does. There are testimonies, witnesses, and advocates along the way if we pay heed. In ancient Israel Elisha was exactly such a teacher, witness, and advocate who noticed the "left behind." He embraced them in ways of restoration. (See Walter Brueggemann, *Testimony to Otherwise: The Witness of Elijah and Elisha*, 2001.) Jesus was such a teacher, witness, and advocate who invested his transformative capacity exactly in the left out in his society. (See Thomas Brodie, *The Crucial Bridge: The Elijah-Elisha Narrative as an Interpretive Synthesis of Genesis-Kings and a Literary Model for the Gospels*, 2000.) We could only draw the conclusion that the church is to be a teacher, witness, and advocate for just such a company. Imagine, if local congregations and their pastors took up their roles of teacher, witness, and advocate, so that the cruel work of dispossession did not go unnoticed and unanswered among us. Such work by the church would require that we face our ignorance that protects our advantage, that we cross from our comfort zones for the sake of such neighbors. But then, nobody has yet suggested that discipleship can be a zone of ignorant comfort. We are given a clue about the fresh learning *even YHWH faced* upon hearing the cries of the slaves!

> Out of their slavery their cry for help rose up to God. God heard their groaning and God remembered his covenant with Abraham, Isaac, and Jacob. God looked upon the Israelites, and God took notice of them…Then the Lord said, "I have observed the misery of my people who are in Egypt; I have heard their cry on account of their taskmasters. Indeed, I know their sufferings, and I have come down to deliver them (Exodus 2:23-25, 3:7-8).

Our awakened sensibility is a first urgent step toward neighborly restoration. It is a step the church makes in its defining vocation. I imagine that Naboth (like the ancient slaves) must have groaned and cried out in great fear and anguish at his execution. Naboth continues to cry out in every verdict of dispossession. His cry sounds among us in many different cadences and in many different dialects, including among us the cadences and dialects of Black Americans. What a work for the church to be listening and responding to that shrill cry!

CHAPTER TEN

On Manning Up

These are among the most chilling, repulsive words I have ever read:

> In the cradle of one white hand, the nigger's privates seemed as remote as meat being weighed in the scales; but seemed heavier, too, much heavier.

They are written by James Baldwin, on his short story, "Going to Meet the Man." They are quoted by Jefferson Cowie, *Freedom's Dominion: A Saga of White Resistance to Federal Power* (2022), in his characterization of a small Alabama town largely defined by white supremacy and racist violence, the town that produced, among others, Governor George Wallace. The words of Baldwin are taken by Cowie to report on the "sexualized ritual of horror" whereby Dr. Walter Britt, the city's most prominent physician, "cut Iver Peterson's testicles from his body" (234-235). Peterson had by his sudden appearance in the dark frightened "a prominent woman" who screamed at the sight of him. That scream was enough to evoke, in the small Alabama town, vigilante who searched for Peterson, found him, and proceeded with the murder of the Black man.

As Baldwin continues his characterization of such a violent act, he writes:

> "The white man stretched them [the private parts], cradled them, caressed them" before the victim "screamed and the crowd screamed as the knife flashed, first up, then down, cutting the dreadful thing away, and the blood came roaring down.

What follows is a lynching by the eager crowd. Cowie narrates:

> The mob then threw a rope around the thick branch of an oak tree and lowered a noose around Iver Peterson's neck as blood poured from his groin. They heaved his body off the ground to break his neck. Dr. Britt was said to be the first to pick up his gun and shoot Iver Peterson's swinging body, and the rest of the mob then followed his lead. So many reports used the words "riddled with bullets" that it had become a cliché of newspaper reporting about lynchings. Their job complete, the mob returned to town and left Iver Peterson's body swinging in the cold air of the leafless winter morning (235).

This violent scene, one often reiterated in the days of rampant lynchings, served to intimidate the Black people, and so sustain a vigorous and uncontested white supremacy. The violence of castration and lynching functioned to assure white control and to complete the degradation of a particular Black man, and by inference Black people in general, who were an imagined threat to white women and white control. Cowie completes his account by reporting that Peterson's brothers avenged Iver Peterson by killing one the vigilante, and so had to flee from the town for their lives. The reported event merits recall in and of itself that serves to remind us of our violent history of racism. The violent killing functions as an act of degradation of a man in order to give credence to White control and Black subservience.

That is enough in itself. Beyond that, I wanted to see what possible linkage I might find with Scripture. My attention was drawn, inescapably, to the Philistines in ancient Israel. During the time of Saul and David, the Philistines constituted a major ongoing threat to Israel. We might judge that the conflict between them was one between *commercial interests* (the Philistines) and *hill country subsis-*

tence farmers (the Israelites). But the clash in the text is articulated differently, as "uncircumcised" and "circumcised"; see Judges 14:13, 15:18, I Samuel 14:6, 17:26, 36, 31:4). Thus, the contrast and distinction is made in terms of a *male ritual marking*. The Philistines constituted a threatening "other" to the Israelites as did Black people to White people in the small Alabama town. While the threat of the Philistines continued for some time, the tension between the two is brought into sharp focus in the dramatic confrontation between Goliath, the Philistine giant, and David, the young Israelite upstart. The words David speaks in the narrative articulate the conflict in theological terms, as the conflict of Whites and Blacks in our society is sometimes given theological expression:

> What shall be done for the man who kills this Philistine, and takes away the reproach from Israel? For who is this uncircumcised Philistine that he should defy the armies of the living God… (I Samuel 17:26)?

> Your servant has killed both lions and bears; and this uncircumcised Philistine shall be like one of them, since he has defied the armies of the living God. The Lord, who saved me from the paw of the lion and from the paw of the bear, will save me from the hand of this Philistine (vv. 36-37).

David's questions go unanswered. His self-certain assertion is enough for Saul to dispatch him into battle. Saul, perhaps with some resignation, can only say, "Go, and may the Lord be with you" (v. 37).

The very next chapter, after the defeat of the Philistine giant, reports on the growing alienation between Saul and David, all initiated by the cunning, scheming Saul. At the outset, Saul imagines that David will have to face the Philistines. Saul sets a trap for David; he proposes to David that he should marry his daughter, Michal. David demurs:

> Does it seem to you a little thing to become the king's son-in-law, seeing that I am a poor man and of no repute? (1 Samuel 18:23)

He does not have the resources required to pay a bride's price. But Saul, in his scheming, is way ahead of David:

> The king desires no marriage present except a hundred foreskins of the Philistines, that he may be avenged on the king's enemies (I Samuel 18:25).

Saul would no doubt be glad to have David kill some number of Philistines. But his intent is otherwise. He anticipates that David's effort at having the Philistine foreskins would lead to David's violent death at the hands of the Philistines. In his answer to Saul, however, David accepts the challenge that Saul offers, ignores Saul's malevolent intent, kills the Philistines, and so qualifies as a fitting match for the daughter of the king:

> David rose and went, along with his men, and killed one hundred of the Philistines; and David brought their foreskins, which were given in full number to the king, that he might become the king's son-in-law (I Samuel 18:27).

The deed is done; the marriage comes to fruition. David has foiled the scheme of Saul, the king who is now his father-in-law.

To be sure, the matter of Philistine "foreskins" is quite incidental to Saul's plot. Nonetheless the narrative depends upon this incidental reality, for seizing the foreskins not only requires the death of the Philistines, but also calls attention to the status of the Philistines as uncircumcised, thus an ominous "other" to the Israelites. The accomplishment of David and the foiling of Saul are reprised in II Samuel 3:14-15:

> Then David sent messengers to Saul's son Ishbaal, saying, "give me my wife Michal, to whom I became engaged at the price of one hundred foreskins of the Philistines." Ishbaal sent and took her from her husband Paltiel the son of Laish (II Samuel 3:14-15).

It occurs to me that *the report from Cowie* and *the narrative of David* have a great deal in common. Both deal with an "other" who is perceived as a threat, Blacks in Alabama and the Philistines in the Holy Land. Both episodes concern an act of violence—sexualized violence—that calls attention to the otherness of the other. Thus the Philistines, not unlike the Blacks, not only suffered violent death, but degradation and humiliation in the loss of their markings of manhood. Both acts lead to "positive" outcomes for the perpetrators of violence. David gets his royal bride; Whites in Alabama reinforce their racist supremacy. The mocking of the manhood of one's enemies is featured in both narratives. It was a triumph in Alabama when Dr. Britt "cradled the nigger's private parts." It must have been a like moment of triumph when David handed the one hundred Philistine foreskins to Saul who had hoped for David's death. In both instances the other is dismissed as vulnerable, despised and, for now, eliminated.

I cannot help but to think that in both narratives there is an exaltation of male power, with the confiscation of the male power (testicles, foreskins) of the humiliated other. The mob in Alabama filled with fear had gone crazy, with a moment of unrestrained white power, as David's violent act marked him as a man sure to win and prevail over Israel's feared and despised enemies.

With the respective preoccupation with *testicles and foreskins*, the two narratives invite reflection on what constitutes manhood. In both narratives, manhood is marked by power, control, and violence.

Among us manhood continues to be marked in such a way concerning some who feel themselves jeopardized by the other. Thus the violence of January 6 and the endless exhibit of Neo-Nazis permit White manhood to be imagined through violence. Such *violence* is enacted as resistance to "replacement"! But of course most of us are not into such performances of violence as a certification of manhood. We may notice, however, two other dimensions of such performed manhood that are close to the surface among us. First, there is the growing evidence of the way in which powerful men have, with impunity, coercively imposed themselves upon vulnerable or needy women. Second, there is little doubt that the regular liturgical performance of the National Football League is an opportunity to observe (and participate in?) the sanctioned violence of football that is generously accompanied by money, male power, and predatory sexuality.

Thus I find in these two repulsive cases of David and Iver Peterson an opportunity to think about manhood in our society. Incidentally I wrote these lines the day after Father's Day, so the matter is otherwise on my mind. Beyond that, I have learned that Father's Day was also the final sermon of Dr. William Barber in his church, Greenleaf Christian Church in Goldsboro, North Carolina before he departed for Yale. In his sermon, Barber focused on being "crippled," as he himself is. He said:

> Your crippledness gives God a chance to show God's strength and it also enables you to be in community, because you cannot do it on your own.

Barber embodies and articulates a very different notion of manhood than that exhibited in our two narratives. In those cases, the manhood of the "other" is erased by violence. Conversely, the manhood of the "winners," (David and Whites) is validated and enhanced. In both cases violence is a ready tool for triumph. Thus:

> Manhood *degraded, denied, erased*;
> Manhood *performed, celebrated, exalted*.

Such *denial* and *exaltation* twinned together of course can have no good, sustainable outcomes, as the "other" persists and endlessly reappears. There is no life without the insistent presence of "the other."

The response we might make to this characterization of manhood from the perspective of our faith is rich and complex. For now I will call attention to only one remarkable usage in the Pauline corpus. In Ephesians 4:13 the writer refers to "maturity":

> ...until all of us come to the unity of the faith and to the knowledge of the Son of God, to maturity, to the measure of the full stature of Christ (Ephesians 4:13).

The term that the NRSV translates as "maturity" in Greek is *andra teleion*, that is, "perfect" or "complete" manliness. The KJV has it:

> ...till we all come to the unity of the faith and to the knowledge of the Son of God, unto a *perfect man*, the measure of the stature of the fullness of Christ.

The chapter goes on to describe "the perfect man" by the measure of Christ. First, there is a description of the "old self" (*palaion anthropon*):

> They are darkened in their understanding, alienated from the life of God because of their ignorance and hardness of heart. They have lost all sensitivity and have abandoned themselves to licentiousness, greedy to practice every kind of impurity...

You were taught to put away your former way of life, your old self, corrupt and deluded by its lusts (Ephesians 4:18-19, 22).

Such a life is contrasted with the "new self" in Christ (*kainon anthropon*):

...to clothe yourselves with the new self, created according to the likeness of God in true righteousness and holiness (v. 24).

The contrast is reiterated in other terms:

Put away from you all bitterness and wrath and anger and wrangling and slander, together with all malice, and be kind to one another, tenderhearted, forgiving one another, as God in Christ has forgiven you (Ephesians 4:30-31).

The old self is characterized by self-indulgence and self-advancement by whatever means necessary. The new self (marked by baptism) has a capacity for forgiveness. Or the same contrast is differently voiced earlier by Paul:

Now the works of the flesh are obvious: fornication, impurity, licentiousness, idolatry, sorcery, enmities, strife, jealousy, anger, quarrels, dissensions, factions, envy, drunkenness, carousing, and things like these...By contrast, the fruit of the Spirit is love, joy, peace, patience, kindness, generosity, faithfulness, gentleness, and self-control. There is no law against such things (Galatians 5:19-23).

In Paul's rendering the matter is a profound *either/or*. It is the business of the community of the baptized to nurture "manhood" that acts out with strength and courage these generative marks of a community of wellbeing in which all members are given due positive regard. In this practice there is no thought or need for degradation or humiliation of anyone else, but rather a readiness and capacity to honor and respect, and therefore to enhance the wellbeing of the other.

Such a way of talking, thinking, and living would have been strange among the members of the mob in Alabama. It would have been equally strange on the horizon of David, who seized the male marking of others as a trophy, and this from the antecedent of our Messiah! In some quarters among us, moreover, such manhood as Paul commends may be perceived as weakness that does not lend itself to the aggressive patriotism so prized among us. The contrast between the "old self" and the "new self" is complete. And while the contrast in Ephesians is cast in terms of maleness, it unambiguously pertains to all of us, whatever our gender markers. Paul does not imagine that he has arrived at such manhood as the new self; such maturity is an ongoing process whereby we may indeed grow toward such maturity:

> Not that I have already obtained this or have already reached the goal; but I press on to make it my own, because Christ Jesus has made me his own. Beloved, I do not consider that I have made it my own; but this one thing I do: forgetting what lies behind and straining forward to what lies ahead, I press on toward the goal for the prize of the heavenly call of God in Christ Jesus. Let those of us then who are mature be of the same mind; and if you think differently about anything, this too God will reveal to you (Philippians 3:12-15).

The term "mature" in verse 15 again translates *teleioi*, "perfect" or "complete." The baptized community is under way in a venture of personhood that boldly contrasts to the toxic models of humanness that are everywhere available in our society. This is indeed a wondrous calling that summons us to daily attentiveness.

CHAPTER ELEVEN

A Revolution Hurried Along

Chris Hedges is among our most passionate truth-tellers who continues his shrill exposé of corporate greed and its costs for our society. I recently went back to his book, *Days of Destruction, Days of Revolt* (2012), written in the wake of the Occupy Wall Street Movement. Happily he is joined in writing this book by Joe Sacco who provides compelling cartoons to go along with the narrative.

Hedges and Sacco consider in turn four case studies of the way in which corporate greed has done its work of destruction, hence, *Days of Destruction*:

- "Days of Theft" (chapter 1) concerns land seizure by the government and speculators from Native Americans;
- "Days of Siege" (chapter 2) considers the hopeless and resourceless in Camden, New Jersey, where the "world is divided between the prey and the predators" (p. 77);
- "Days of Devastation" (chapter 3) tells of the ruin of the land in West Virginia by the coal companies, and the local society is left completely bereft and without hope;
- "Days of Slavery" (chapter 4) narrates the plight of Latino camps where the laborers live in sub-human conditions in order to grow the vegetables needed for consumer tables.

These chapters are very disturbing reading. Each of these chapters features an economy that has been ransacked by corporate greed with the working community left behind and abandoned, without power and without hope.

The second part of their study concerns a popular uprising that will overcome the power of corporate greed and return power to the people (chapter 5). They regard Occupy Wall Street as a harbinger of the revolution that is sure to come when enough people decide they are no longer willing to live in the "cages" of corporate greed. "Power to the people" is the certain antidote to power in the hands of the few that manage to reduce too many people into willing docile conformity.

It is my wont, as regularly as I am able, to read such contemporary analysis at an interface with a biblical text. It is my conviction that reading at that intersection has a chance to illuminate both the biblical text and the contemporary writing. In this instance I propose to read Hedges and Sacco alongside the text in II Kings 9-10 that is also very disturbing reading. This biblical text, violent as it is, is never read in church, and in general is neglected. I have no doubt that attention must be paid to it for the reasons I will suggest. Reading these two chapters in the Bible knowingly requires recognition of these two critical awarenesses:

1. Every God comes along with a socioeconomic political option that the God champions and legitimates. This defining linkage is elemental for reading this text. The linkage is well said in the aphorism of Karl Marx:

> The criticism of heaven is thus transformed into the criticism of earth, the criticism of religion into the criticism of law, and the criticism of theology into the criticism of politics.

Thus for example, there is no doubt that YHWH the God of Israel, since the Exodus emancipation, comes along with a neighborly covenantal economy that YHWH champions and legitimates.

2. In this text and in the Bible generally, Baal is the legitimator and champion of a socioeconomic system that practices predatory greed and individual wealth at the expense of the community. From this awareness it follows that the deep contestation between *YHWH and Baal* (for example in the narrative of Mt. Carmel (I Kings 18) is at the same time a deep contestation between *a neighborly covenantal economy and an economy of predatory greed and individual wealth* (as for example in the narrative of I Kings 21). Thus the issue joined in II Kings 9-10 is not unlike the issue joined by Hedges and Sacco in their analysis of destruction and their anticipation of revolution.

The biblical text is divided into two parts. II Kings 9:1-13 is the preparation for and initiation of the revolution to be led by Jehu. What follows in 9:14-10:28 is the cunning, bloody implementation of the revolution with an outcome of the installation of a new government led by the leader of the revolt, Jehu. The initiation of the revolution is credited to Elisha. This is the same Elisha who in previous narratives had stood outside of and apart from the royal regime, manifesting and performing a transformative power that could not be understood or curbed by the royal regime. Now Elisha moves to overthrow the Omride dynasty that he has long since rejected. This dramatic movement toward new governance is through three-fold reiteration of the same formula:

Elisha instructs a member of his circle:

Thus says the Lord: I anoint you king over Israel (v. 3).

Elisha's messenger says to Jehu with oil poured over his head,

Thus says the Lord the God of Israel, I anoint you king over the people of the Lord, over Israel (v. 6).

Jehu reports to his companion soldiers, quoting the messenger,

Thus says the Lord, I anoint you king over Israel (v. 12).

The formulation is the same in each case. Except that it is worth noting that in the second iteration of that formula, it is filled out by the added phrases, "the God of Israel," and "the people of the Lord." This double intensification, at the moment of anointing, is surely to accent that for both God and people the anointing concerns the creation of a covenantal community that is in sharp contrast to the present governance of the Omride dynasty. It does not worry Elisha or the messenger or Jehu himself or the acclaiming troops that there is no vacancy in the royal office. They know that full well. They also know full well that their act of anointing and acclaiming amounts to a resolve to overthrow established authority that is now viewed by them as illegitimate. The reason for their readiness to do the overthrow of established authority is that it is a dynasty committed to the practice of Baalism.

In the second part of the narrative, the theme is the progressive advance of new governance, the implementation of the anointing (II Kings 9:14-10:28). First Jehu must deal with the present kings, Joram in Israel and Ahaziah in Judah (9:14-29). It is ironically dramatic that Jehu kills Joram exactly on the erstwhile property of Naboth the Jezreelite, thus identifying the revolution with the peasants who have been done in by the predatory practices of the Omride dynasty. In short order King Ahaziah of Judah is also slain (vv. 27-29). Then follows the dramatic disposal of Jezebel, now the queen mother, again with an allusion to the Naboth murder (vv. 30-37; see I Kings 21:17-19). Thus the royal house is decimated, and the revolution is staged with a full and ready identification with Naboth who is a stand-in for the peasants who have suffered at the hands of the predatory rulers.

Tucked into this narrative is the verse that has kept Jehu famous. "He drives like a maniac" (II Kings 9:20). Or as we now say, "He drives like Jehu." Jehu is in a huge hurry. He knows that his revolution is urgent. He knows that as long as the present regime lasts the vulnerable suffer. We may take his urgency as a measure of the catastrophe wrought by the regime, a catastrophe that is matched by our own current corporate greed. It is for us, as for Jehu, a time of acute urgency.

In chapter 10 the seizure of power by the new peasant movement is completed. First Jehu kills seventy sons of Ahab in Samaria (10:1-11). This massive number of princes no doubt in popular perception represented extravagant self-indulgence that contrasted with the subsistence economy of the peasants. Yet again the killing is linked to the word of Elijah concerning Naboth:

> Know then that there shall fall to the earth nothing of the word of the Lord, which the Lord spoke concerning the house of Ahab; for the Lord has done what he said through his servant Elijah (II Kings 10:10).

Then follows the complete wipeout of the royal family of Judah, forty-two persons in all; he spared none of them (vv. 12-14). Thus in both 9:27-29 and 10:12-14 the disposal of the Southern royal family seems almost an afterthought to the narrator.

In the reprise of 10:15-17 we are given yet another notation about the remainder of the royal family in Samaria with another reference to Elijah. But then, in some relief from the killing, Jehu welcomes to his company Jehonadab son of Rechab. We know elsewhere that the "Rechabites" are an embodiment of the old tribal, covenantal ways who have resisted the high-life extravagance of the royal house (Jeremiah 35:1-19). Jehu identifies his movement with the most old-fashioned conservatism in Israel, thus providing important credentialing for his movement.

In the final paragraph of the narrative Jehu conducts a mop-up action against the followers of Baal (10:18-28). These verses are filled with references to Baal, the legitimator and champion of the predatory economy of the Omrides:

> Jehu summoned all the *prophets of Baal*, all his worshipers, and all his priests (v. 19).
> Jehu cunningly planned to destroy all the *worshipers of Baal* (v. 19).
> Jehu ordered a *solemn assembly for Baal* (v. 20).
> The *temple of Baal* was filled from wall to wall (v. 21).
> Jehu ordered that the vestments for the *worshipers of Baal* be brought out (v. 22).
> Jehu, along with Jehonadab the Rechabite, made sure there were no worshipers of YHWH among *the throng of Baal worshipers* (v.23).
> They burned *the pillar of Baal* (v. 26).
> They destroyed *the temple of Baal* and made it a latrine (v. 27).

And then in conclusion:

> Thus Jehu *wiped out Baal* from Israel (28).

Jehu's action is full, complete, and final. The events set in motion by Elijah have come to fulfillment! The narrative leaves us in no doubt that the intent of Jehu is to overrun and eliminate the political economy legitimated by Baal. He does so on behalf of the peasant economy represented by Naboth, voiced by Elijah, performed by Elisha, and embodied by Jehonadab the Rechabite.

We must of course take care to notice the massive violence of Jehu. There is no way around that accent in the narrative. But we must also notice that the initiating violence did not come from Jehu, but from Ahab, Jezebel, and the followers of Baal. (See Dom Helder Camara, *The Spiral of Violence*). That regime in Samaria was, from its inception to its implementation and demise, an act of violence against resourceless peasants. The responding violence of Jehu may seem disproportionate until we take into account the long-running wholesale systemic violence of the regime.

The parallel to the destruction and revolution of Hedges and Sacco seems unavoidably evident. As the Omride dynasty had severely exploited the peasant community, so the predatory economy of corporate greed had worked its violent deathliness against Native Americans, the inner city vulnerable, coal miners, and Hispanics, and any others who were useful targets for exploitation. Like the strange movement of Jehu, the Occupy Wall Street Movement came from outside the sphere and reach of the regime and had on its side the urgent need of nameless unnumbered persons.

We have on our hands this dangerous biblical text. There is good reason we avoid it in practice, in the first instance because it is filled with violence. But the deeper reason we avoid it is that it is a *rendering of a revolution from below on behalf of the resourceless*. It takes no stretch of the imagination to see that the Jesus movement, in a very different mode, continued that revolution that proved so dangerous to the establishment that it ended in a state execution.

The primary learning here, as I see it, is the deep link between *the God-claim of the gospel* and *the socioeconomic political by-product* of that God-claim. YHWH always comes with a neighborly covenantal economy. Jesus always comes with a caring eye for those left behind. The Trinitarian God is marked by suffering and communal solidarity so that this God can never be easily at home with predatory wealth or the system of usurpation. Every time a preacher or a teacher of the church speaks up, she must willy-nilly bear witness to *the byproduct of neighborliness.* This God never travels but with the vulnerable. We prefer to have "only God." But the God of the gospel is not on offer in that way. That is why Jesus insisted that we cannot have only one "great commandment." There are always two (Mark 12: 28-34)! *Always God and neighbor,* both loved passionately and urgently. The Occupy Wall Street Movement fully understood this, even if in a very different idiom. Nonetheless, we may finally trust the idiom we have been given: "God and neighbor." Elijah knew this in his severity. Elisha knew this as he performed among the outsiders. Jehonadab the Rechabite never forgot it. And Jehu acted it out in the face of systemic violence.

The biblical narrative is honest enough, in its highly stylized conclusion to Jehu, to recognize that the movement could last only so long:

> The Lord said to Jehu, "Because you have done well in carrying out what I consider right, and in accordance with all that was in my heart have dealt with the house of Ahab, your sons of the fourth generation shall sit on the throne of Israel" (II Kings 10:30).

Only four generations, a short shelf life: only Jehu, Jehoahaz, Jehoash, and the great Jeroboam II. Not more! Even this eager movement is not perfect:

> But Jehu was not careful to follow the law of the Lord the God of Israel with all his heart; he did not turn from the sins of Jeroboam, which he caused Israel to commit (v. 31).

We get an imperfect movement. Even that, however, is well worth the effort. The effort must be made.

CHAPTER TWELVE

Fear of the Unnumbered "Other"

Concerning "replacement theory," work backward in time. Most of us were quite unaware of "replacement theory" until the violent uprising in Charlottesville. There the marching, violent chanters asserted, "We will not be replaced." Their imagined threat of "replacement" came variously from unnamed dangers, or more particularly "the Jews." Either way, the march exhibited pseudo-victims making a defense of white America. The marchers who chanted gave vent to their alienation from society, and their refusal or inability to accommodate the changing socioeconomic reality of our culture. Needless to say, their chant and the violence that ensued did not alter that changing reality; they only permitted a momentary exhibit of fear-cum-hate. But the exhibition could appeal, as we have discovered, to a long-running theory that the white population of our nation is in jeopardy and requires protective advantage.

Behind the Charlottesville chanters is the theoretical work of a French scholar, Renaud Camus. His book *Le Grand Remplacement,* in 2011, provided a basis from which practical protests concerning "replacement" could be mounted. As I noted in my piece, "The Great Replacement," behind Camus (though likely unrecognized by Camus) is the work of France Amasa Walker, a long-time influential policymaker in Washington, D.C. Walker

> developed the "displacement" principle. This principle states that immigration does not add to the total population because the amount of immigration is offset by the fall of the birth

In God We Do Not Trust 93

rate of the native population. Immigration merely results in the substitution of the foreign born for the native population (Bernard Newton, *The Economics of Francis Amass Walker: American Economics in Transition*, 1968, 143).

Walker developed this theory because,

> large numbers of Eastern and Southern Europeans were entering the nation, and Walker was alarmed because he believed that these people (through no fault of their own), were of a lower economic, political, and cultural level (145).

Walker explained the fall of the national birthrate with this judgment:

> The American shrank from the industrial competition thus thrust upon him. He was unwilling himself to engage the lowest kind of day-labor with these new elements of the population; and he was even more unwilling to bring sons and daughters into the world to enter into that competition. In effect, then, immigration did not represent a net addition to the total population, but the substitution of native stock with foreign peoples (146).

That is, the arrival and threat of these "foreigners" caused a drop in the birthrate of the Euro-white US population. Newton concludes this report on Walker with the summary statement that most subsequent discussions find this replacement theory to be "of limited validity"; "the result of modern research has been to throw serious doubt on the validity of the Walker theory" (150). The matter of "limited validity" and "serious doubt," however, has not precluded appeal to it, as we have seen in Charlottesville.

While Camus is widely credited with the contemporary emergence of "replacement theory," Newton surprisingly reports that the theory was "foreshadowed" already by none other than Benjamin Franklin, the most senior of our founding fathers. Newton reports that already in 1751 Franklin wrote:

> The importation of foreigners into a country, that has as many inhabitants as the present employments and provisions for subsistence will bear, will be in the end no increase of people; unless the newcomers have more industry and frugality than the natives, and then they will provide more subsistence, and increase in the country; but they will gradually eat the natives out (147-148).

Like many others Franklin has no hesitation in labeling Euro-Americans as "natives." We must conclude that the theory, in tacit but menacing ways, has been present and operative amid our republican conversations from the outset of our nation. It is not fashionable to voice the theory, but it is there waiting to enforce our most elemental fears of the other.

In my consideration of scripture my fresh insight concerning this matter of "replacement" is to push back to the earliest moments of the Exodus narrative. The Exodus narrative begins with this affirmation:

> But the Israelites were fruitful and prolific; they multiplied and grew exceedingly strong, so that the land was filled with them (Exodus 1:7).

The narrative reports on the actualization of the promise God had made to father Abraham:

> He brought him outside and said, "Look toward the heavens and count the stars, if you are able to count them." Then he said to him, "So shall your descendents be" (Genesis 15:5).

The Israelites are destined to be prolific according to the blessing of God. Consequently, Exodus 1:15-22 reports a crisis in Egypt due to the vigorous child-bearing of the Hebrew women. The narrative stages a contest between *the fear of Pharaoh* and *the fruitfulness of the Hebrew women*, or alternatively, between *the fear of Pharaoh* and *the skill of the Hebrew midwives*. Either way, Pharaoh decrees the death of Hebrew baby boys whom he perceives as a threat. His decree is curious because the birth of Hebrew babies provided a greater slave workforce for Pharaoh; but his fear outran his economic interest. The narrative, however, refuses and contradicts the decree of Pharaoh. The adversative "but" in verse 17 avers that Pharaoh's decree cannot stand. It cannot stand because the Hebrew midwives feared God and did not fear Pharaoh. It did not stand

> because the Hebrew women are not like the Egyptian women;
> for they are vigorous and give birth before the midwife comes
> to them (Exodus 1:19).

The contrast between the Hebrew women and the Egyptian women is an anticipation of the judgment of Walker concerning the contrast of US immigrant women and the women of the settled white population. The result is that "the people multiplied and became very strong" (v. 20).

When we look closely at the motivation of Pharaoh and his fearful action, we may find a hint of his motivation in the notice of the Genesis narrative:

> The Egyptians could not eat with the Hebrews, for that is an abomination to the Egyptians (Genesis 43:32).

The Egyptians regarded the Hebrews as second-rate, second-class, inferior, and ritually unclean. For the governing population of Egypt, the Hebrew people are a dispensable resource and repellent presence. The narrative of Exodus 1:15-22, however, is told from an Israelite perspective. The very population threatened by Pharaoh is seen to be the carrier of God's blessing, and consequently the wave of the future. It takes little imagination to see how this ancient contrast became the seedbed for what follows. Every established population and every established regime regards itself as legitimate, and thus sees any impingement upon its governance, wealth, or territory as a dangerous, unacceptable threat. Behind every such discernment, as with Pharaoh is a tacit assumption of superiority. It was so for Pharaoh, as it was so for Franklin, for Walker, for Camus, and for the mob at Charlottesville. The measure of the threat may determine the measure of readiness for violence in the defense of the old established order of privilege and advantage, a defense that reached a violent, lethal peak in Charlottesville.

Thus the Bible stands as the fountainhead of the readiness of a "superior" people to act decisively against other peoples judged to be inferior. It did not take long, in the biblical telling, for matters to be inverted so that *the Hebrew slaves* abruptly became *the "Holy People"* with a warrant to replace the Canaanites and their despicable gods. The rest, from that moment forward, is "history."

We may, from the Exodus narrative, quickly read forward. When we read forward, the discriminatory judgments of Franklin, Walker, and Camus all make good sense. Along that way forward, we will notice that the Exodus narrative is reiterated by Matthew with King Herod now cast in the role of Pharaoh:

> When Herod saw that he had been tricked by the wise men, he was infuriated, and he sent and killed all the children in and around Bethlehem who were two years old or under, according to the time that he had learned from the wise men (Matthew 2:16).

Herod did indeed fear *replacement*. He feared replacement by the new "King of the Jews." And so he readily undertook the violence that he thought would keep his place secure. It was violence readily reperformed for the same reason at Charlottesville. The weeping of mother Rachel concerns exactly the loss of the beloved children of the Hebrews at the hand of Herod who feared and fended off replacement:

> Then was fulfilled what had been spoken through the prophet Jeremiah:
> A voice was heard in Ramah, wailing and loud lamentation,
> Rachel weeping for her children;
> she refused to be comforted, because they are no more (Matthew 2:17-18).

(On Rachel's jeopardized children, see Jonathan Kozol, *Rachel and Her Children: Homeless Families in America*.) Matthew reports that the son of Mary and Joseph was protected from Herod's violent assault by the agency of an angel. Clearly not all of the children of Rachel are so protected by angels. When we move forward through the works I have cited, we come eventually to Margaret Atwood's *The Handmaid's Tale*; in that narrative the main character in the plot is recruited for reproductive purposes, because the governing regime is incapable of such reproduction.

The sweep of this theme from the ancient Hebrew midwives, Shiphrah and Puah, to Atwood and Charlottesville, is breathtaking. It is everywhere and every time a story of a *frightened establishment* of privilege and advantage and *a generative force "from below"* that is seen as a threat to the establishment. The several responses of the frightened establishment is, determinedly, to belittle and diminish the population that is perceived as a threat, to reduce them to sub-human status and so ineligible for power, wealth, or wellbeing.

The "other" that is seen as a threat always appears to be excessively numerous, and so needing to be curbed by whatever means that is necessary. It is worth noting that in Exodus 12:38, the company departing Egypt is reported as "a mixed multitude" ('rv rv), that is, a mass beyond count. The establishment is grossly outnumbered or is perceived to be outnumbered.

In the imagination of Israel, Egypt continues to be the paradigmatic menace that had begun already with the ancient Pharaoh. This way of defining Egypt as enemy and threat receives its extreme articulation in the oracles of Ezekiel 29:1-12, 30:2-26, and 32:1-21). Remarkably, Ezekiel can also anticipate a time to come when YHWH will rehabilitate Egypt in its own land (29:3-15). That rehabilitation, however, is limited and circumscribed:

> It shall be the most lowly of the kingdoms, and never again exalt itself above the nations; and I will make them so small that they will never again rule over the nations. The Egyptians shall never again be the reliance of the house of Israel; they will recall their iniquity, when they turned to them for aid. Then they shall know that I am the Lord God (Ezekiel 29:15-16).

The restoration of Egypt is to national identity, but not ever again to expansive power.

It remained, however, for the prophet Isaiah, to utter a final word in the Old Testament concerning Egypt. In a familiar mode Isaiah anticipates massive divine judgment against Egypt (Isaiah 19:1-17). But then, in a remarkable reversal, Isaiah anticipates the complete restoration of Egypt, not as a menacing superpower, but as a legitimate partner in the affairs of the nations. That is, the Egyptians will now, at long last, accept the sovereign rule of YHWH:

> It will be a sign and a witness to the Lord of hosts in the land of

Egypt; when they cry to the Lord because of oppressors, he will send them a savior, and will defend and deliver them. The Lord will make himself known to the Egyptians; and the Egyptians will know the Lord on that day, and will worship with sacrifice and burnt offering, and they will make vows to the Lord and perform them. The Lord will strike Egypt, striking and healing; they will return to the Lord, and he will listen to their supplications and heal them (Isaiah 19:20-22).

And then this remarkable affirmative conclusion:

> On that day there will be a highway from Egypt to Assyria, and the Assyrians will come into Egypt, and the Egyptians into Assyria, and the Egyptians will worship with the Assyrians. On that day Israel will be the third with Egypt and Assyria, a blessing in the midst of the earth, whom the Lord of hosts has blessed, saying, Blessed be Egypt my people, and Assyria the work of my hands, and Israel my heritage (Isaiah 19:23-25).

Not only will Egypt be restored among the nations but Egypt will become a chosen people of YHWH: "*Egypt my people*" (v. 25). Egypt will not monopolize that status of "chosen," but will share it along with its long-running rivals and enemies, Assyria and Israel. Seen in the context of "replacement theory," the prophet anticipates a time when those who face replacement and those who pose a threat of replacing can come together, reconciled by the rule of YHWH, the Lord of the covenant. The anticipation is breathtaking.

In the belated utterance of the prophet, all the violence of Egypt is overridden. All the fear that Egypt had of the slave community is ended. All the divine judgment against it is over. There is a peaceable settlement among the erstwhile enemies that permits peace in their part of the world.

It is exactly the prophetic claim that the work of YHWH is reconciliation between would-be replacers and would-be replaced. It follows exactly that the prophetic work of the church is to anticipate such reconciliation between the *would-be replaced* and the *would-be replacers*. When we seek an analogue of this anticipated reconciliation in the New Testament, we of course find concerning the long-running tension between Jews and Gentiles. Before very long, the inclusiveness of Paul will prevail over the scruples of James. The matter is anticipated by Peter:

> I truly understand that God shows no partiality, but in every nation anyone who fears him and does what is right is acceptable to him (Acts 10:34-35).

The matter is given nuance by James:

> Therefore I have reached the decision that we should not trouble those Gentiles who are turning to God, but we should write to them to abstain only from things polluted by idols and from fornication and from whatever has been strangled, and from blood (Acts 15:19-20).

This apostolic decision permits the grand lyrical conclusion of the epistle:

> For he is our peace; in his flesh he has made both groups into one and has broken down the dividing wall, that is, the hostility between us. He has abolished the law with its commandments and ordinances, that he might create in himself one new humanity in place of the two, thus making peace, and might reconcile both groups to God in one body through the cross, thus putting to death that hostility through it. So he came and proclaimed peace to you who were far off and peace to those

who were near; for through him both of us have access in one Spirit to the Father. So then you are no longer strangers and aliens, but you are citizens with the saints and also members of the household of God, built upon the foundation of the apostles and prophets, with Christ Jesus himself as the cornerstone. In him the whole structure is joined together and grows into a holy temple in the Lord; in whom you also are built together spiritually into a dwelling place for God (Ephesians 2:14-22).

The apostolic settlement has come a very long way from the struggle of the would-be replaced and the would-be replacers. That long way, nonetheless, can be traversed with patience and generosity. The wondrous oracle of Isaiah leaves no doubt that God's great transformative reach readily overrides our fearful divisiveness. In the moment, however, nothing is denied about the alienation. It is all acknowledged, a first step toward shared restoration.

CHAPTER THIRTEEN

Divine Genocide

A long while ago I had lunch with a new friend, a distinguished Jewish scholar of religion at Emory University. In our lunch conversation we talked some about our common concern about Israel and the land of promise. And then he said, "I wish all Palestinians were dead." He had no sense of irony or embarrassment about his statement. I was too shocked and dumbfounded to say anything in response.

That conversation has led me to reflect on the biblical testimony to *herem*, the biblical notion that what belongs to God must be offered as a burnt offering with nothing held back in reserve from God. The term *herem* is closely linked to our term "harem," the notion that women will be devoted singularly to the wants and needs of the king. Thus the term can be translated as "devoted," but since it involves a sacrifice of burning, it is also rendered as "utterly destroy" or "exterminate." The oldest usage of the term in the Bible has to do with the worship of other gods that detracts from the singular sovereignty of YHWH:

> Whoever sacrifices to any god, other than the Lord alone, shall be *devoted to destruction* (Exodus 22:20).

This claim is reiterated in Deuteronomy 13:12-18 with the term reiterated in verses 16-17:

> All of its spoil you shall gather into its public square; then burn the town and all of its spoil with fire, as a *whole burnt offering*

to the Lord your God. It shall remain a perpetual ruin, never to be rebuilt. Do not let anything devoted to destruction stick to your hand, so that the Lord may turn from his fierce anger and show you compassion, and in his compassion multiply you, as he swore to our ancestors (Deuteronomy 13:16-17).

That usage concerning YHWH's sovereignty, however, easily morphed into land seizure, since the land of promise was regarded as "holy to YHWH," a status that required the destruction of all of the inhabitants of the land who did not worship YHWH. Thus already "in the wilderness," the term is used at Hormah (The name of the site consists in the same three root letters as *herem* = "destruction"):

> Then Israel made a vow to the Lord and said, "If you will indeed give this people into our hands, then we will *utterly destroy* their towns." The Lord listened to the voice of Israel, and handed over the Canaanites; and they *utterly destroyed* them and their towns; so the place was called Hormah (Numbers 21:2-3).

With the entry into the land the term pertains, in turn to Jericho (Joshua 6:17, 21), Hazor (Joshua 11:11-12, 20-21), Sihon (Deuteronomy 2:34), Og (Deuteronomy 3:6), Makkedah (Joshua 10:28), Eglon (Joshua 10:34-35), Hebron (Joshua 10:36-37), Debir (Joshua 10:39), and eventually the whole land (Joshua 10:40). In a quite stylized way the term is applied to the "seven nations," that is, all the non-Israelite peoples:

> —the Hittites, the Girgashites, the Amorites, the Canaanites, the Perizzites, the Hivites, and the Jebusites, seven nations mightier and more numerous than you—and when the Lord your God gives them over to you and you defeat them, then

you must *utterly destroy* them. Make no covenant with them and show no mercy (Deuteronomy 7:1-2). You shall *annihilate* them—the Hittites and the Amorites, the Canaanites and the Perizzites, the Hivites and the Jebusites—just as the Lord your God has commanded (Deuteronomy 20:17).

The latter usage is intensified by an infinitive absolute. The claim is made that all those who do not worship YHWH are idolaters, and so are to be offered up to YHWH in what is taken to be an act of uncompromising obedience by Israel. In highly stylized ways, even prophetic poetry can belatedly assert the rule of YHWH over the nations through such destruction:

> For the Lord is enraged against all the nations,
> and furious against all their hoards;
> he has *doomed* them, has given them over to slaughter (Isaiah 34:2).

> Go up to the land of Merathaim;
> go up against her,
> and attack the inhabitants of Pekod
> and utterly destroy the last of them, says the Lord;
> do all that I have commanded you...
> Come against her from every quarter;
> open her granaries;
> pile her up like heaps of grain,
> and *destroy her utterly*;
> let nothing be left of her (Jeremiah 50:21, 26).

It is clear that such radical obedience both requires and gives warrant for Israel to destroy its enemies in violent, wholesale ways that are justified as obedience to the rigorous demands of YHWH for singular loyalty. The equation of "idolatry" with illicit "land occupation" provides motivation for Israel's relentless violence.

There is one other text that takes up the matter of *herem*. The extended narrative in I Samuel 15 suggests a closure to or an emancipation from the notion of "utterly destroy" in obedience to YHWH:

> Now go and attack Amalek, and utterly destroy all that they have; do not spare them, but kill both man and woman, child and infant, ox and sheep, camel and donkey (I Samuel 15:3).

This command is congruent with the command of Deuteronomy 25:17-19 that occupies the final, ultimate position in the law corpus of Deuteronomy. We may, in these texts, take the Amalekites as the paradigmatic enemy of Israel. Saul obeys the command of Samuel and utterly destroys the Amalekites, except that he spares King Agag and the best of what was valuable: sheep, cattle, fatlings, and lambs. That is, he compromised the command and did not fully obey the instruction to do *herem*. Saul declares his obedience to Samuel:

> May you be blessed by the Lord; I have carried out the command of the Lord (I Samuel 15:13).

But Samuel, in his vigilance, detects that Saul has compromised his command to do *herem* (v. 14). Saul promptly blames his compromise on the people:

> They have brought them from the Amalekites; for the people spared the best of the sheep and the cattle, to sacrifice to the Lord our God; but the rest we have utterly destroyed (v. 15).

Samuel reiterates his command:

> And the Lord sent you on a mission, and said, "Go, *utterly destroy* the sinners, the Amalekites, and fight against them until they are consumed" (v. 18).

Saul pleads his innocence, but Samuel is uncompromising and unforgiving. Samuel himself kills Agag (v. 33). And he declares that "the Lord has taken the kingdom of Israel from you this very day" (v. 28). That is, the violation of *herem* is so serious that it bespeaks the end of Saul's rule. We may judge that Saul's action was a move away from old tribal practice to a more "rational" approach to governance. But Samuel, with his immense authority, defends the old practice and insists upon the most radical Yahwism he can muster. The confrontation is between two modes of governance and here the old tribal order prevails.

> Samuel did not see Saul again until the day of his death, but Samuel grieved over Saul. And the Lord was sorry that he had made Saul king over Israel (I Samuel 15:35).

The meaning, extremity, violence, and specificity of *herem* are fully clear in this array of texts. The notion of *herem* justifies extreme violence against Israel's enemies according to the will of YHWH. That is, we have nothing less than a *divinely ordered habit of genocide*. According to this provision, YHWH is uncompromising in a demand for sovereignty. Consequently, the Land of Promise, that is holy to YHWH and given to Israel as a possession, must be purged of all idolaters. The usage reflects a stunning combination of *divine sovereignty* and *land provision* for the chosen people.

The meaning of the practice is clear. The more difficult question is what to make of it in our interpretation. When one is completely committed to the cause of the state of Israel, the matter is not problematic. Thus Shlomo Avineri, an Israeli political scientist, can assert with great innocence:

> From the point of view of mankind's humanistic morality we were wrong to take the land from the Canaanites. There is only

one catch. The command of God ordered us to be the people of the land of Israel.

While that judgment may reassure some, many other interpreters, including Jewish interpreters, are bothered by such divinely ordered violence, and so the inclination of scholars is to tone down the matter to say that *herem* is exaggerated, fictional, or metaphorical:

- It is *exaggerated*. While there was some violence required for occupation, it was never wholesale or comprehensive.

- It is *fictional*. Such violence never happened, but it is asserted in order to connect land-taking to YHWH.

- It is *metaphorical*. It is not to be taken literally, but is only violence that is textually performed.

What is lacking in such a detoxification of the text is recognition that the image of *herem* is shot through with ideology, that is, reality distorted on behalf of a specific interest. In his wise exposition from a while ago, Patrick Miller notices the ideological component in Israel's historical memory:

> The roots of ideology in Israelite thought are to be found in the earliest period, particularly in the election and covenant theology of Israel. A fully articulated and worked-out ideology, however, does not really manifest itself until the Yahwist's presentation of Israel's history when it becomes considerably retrospective. The notion of a chosen people and the belief in divine promises, which are at the center of his interpretation, contain almost by definition ideological qualities. For here is a group, in this case an ethnic and later national group, pictured as bound together in common cause, assuming for ideologi-

cal reasons a common origin, Abraham, and having moved toward a common goal—the "utopia" of the Promised Land. In this context faith and ideology are closely intertwined (Patrick Miller, "Faith and Ideology in the Old Testament," *Israelite Religion and Biblical Theology: Collected Essays* (2000, p. 634).

Miller, moreover, specifically links the matter of ideology to the tradition of *herem*:

> An important element in Israel's early sacral wars and in the ideology growing out of them was *herem*, the ban, according to which the booty and captives were consecrated to Yahweh and totally destroyed....Thus in light of the later situation the role of the *herem* in Israel is reinterpreted, giving it a more significant and fundamental place and transforming the early conflict of the conquest into a forthright *Religionskampf* with the *herem* at the center as a divine command to avoid Canaanite contamination. The real purposes of the *herem* and the conflicts have been covered over as an ideological interpretation of Israel's beginnings has developed....The 'gift' of the land to Israel is for two reasons: (1) Yahweh loves Israel (Deut. 7:8); and (2) Yahweh is driving out the nations because of their wickedness (Deut. 9:5). There can be little doubt that Israel or elements within Israel took the last reason at face value and were convinced both of the accuracy of the statement and the legitimacy of Yahweh's action. But the ideological acquisition of the needed land cannot be ascribed to its own faithfulness, and it is apparently not enough to say that Yahweh gives the land out of love. The present occupants of the land (i.e. prior to Israel's occupation) are wicked and deserve to lose the land through divine wrath although one might be hard-pressed to prove the greater wickedness of the Amorites, Canaanites, Girgashites, Perizites, and so on (Miller 640-41, 643).

There can be no doubt that Israel's justification for land seizure, whatever the historicity of "the conquest," is permeated with self-serving congratulations. That ideological force made it possible to connect *Israel's eagerness for land* with the *savage rule of YHWH*. While it is impossible to sort out the ingredients of "faith" and "ideology," there can be no doubt of an element of self-serving in the ideology of *herem*. The outcome of such self-justification on the one hand is that it gave Israel full authorization for the wholesale violence against its neighbors. On the other hand, and more seriously, it implicates YHWH in the practice. YHWH now has a partisan partner in Israel for the enactment of violence on a grand scale. It is certain that we are not permitted innocence in the matter, not even by the most fervent Israelite interpreters of the Old Testament.

Thus we may choose to deal with the presence of *herem* in the text by concluding that the matter is exaggerated, fictional, or metaphorical. But there the evidence stands in the text, ready to be taken up by later generations of interpreters for various nefarious purposes. It may be that *herem* was never an actuality for ancient Israel. But now, in our contemporary circumstance, we are witnessing something like *herem* as Israel conducts its violent assaults on Gaza. On the day I write this, the number of murdered Gazan inhabitants is 21,300. The assault of Hamas against Israel on October 7 is horrendous and unacceptable, and Israel has a right to defend itself. Israel's response to that violence, however, is disproportionate and amounts to nothing less than *herem*, a wholesale slaughter of enemies for the purpose of securing the land of promise. And while the announced purpose of the onslaught in Gaza is to kill Hamas, one might readily suspect that in fact the intent is, to echo my friend from Emory University, to kill every Palestinian. Thus the "collateral damage" enacted by Israeli forces is without restraint or limit. The Israeli military is without restraint or discipline. Such action is taken to be fully justified by the Israeli government. Indeed the government of Netanyahu might decide, echoing Shlomo Avis, "there is only one catch." Such a sentiment is breathtaking in its "innocence." It is all the more breathtaking when it comes to reality in the form of dead Gazan inhabitants. The scene of slain Gazans is a reiteration of the conclusion to Israel's ancient tale of emancipation:

> Thus the Lord saved Israel that day from the Egyptians; and Israel saw the Egyptians dead on the seashore (Exodus 14:30).

Methinks it is the work of faithful preaching and faithful teaching to make visible the deep, deep contradiction that is offered in the Bible between the force of violence attributed to YHWH and our inclination to stress and embrace the claims for Yahweh's generous love. Adjudication of this contradiction is the hard, inescapable, insoluble work of interpretation.

Before we finish, we may pause to ask whether Israel in its seeking and claiming the land of promise might have had an alternative to such unrestrained violence. Perhaps we may find a clue in the harsh command of Moses:

> You shall devour all the peoples that the Lord your God is giving over to you, show them no pity (Deuteronomy 7:16; see also Joshua 11:20).

The practice of *herem* is exactly and precisely the exhibit of "no mercy." Thus the alternative to *herem* is likely to be *mercy (rhm)*. The claim of divine mercy looms large in Israel's covenantal rhetoric. Such a divine inclination might indeed be performed in the life of the world. It is possible to imagine, against the record, that Israel might have practiced mercy toward other inhabitants of the land. In the ancient world Israel might have curbed its violence by mercy, but mostly it did not.

So now, the state of Israel might show mercy toward Palestinians, enough mercy that acknowledges and permits the full life of the Palestinian community. In the end it is only such mercy that will make a just peace possible in Israel or anywhere else. In the end, it is the same with the United States. It is possible that White people in the United States might show mercy on Native Peoples and Black people, sufficient mercy that permits them, like White people, to have a fully empowered prospect for a human future. The elimination of "the other" cannot ever succeed. It is recorded that the *herem* of Israel could not fully eliminate the other peoples. (See Judges 1:27-33 with the repeated refrain, "did not drive out.") So it is with us. A very different practice is required and is possible, a practice that might lead to generous policies and neighborly practices. The unlearning of *herem* toward "the other" is a lesson upon which the church must relentlessly insist. In the end, Israel's attraction to YHWH is one of mercy, the very mercy that refuses violence toward neighbors.

EPILOGUE

'Tis the Season to be Violent!

We eagerly anticipate that Christmas will be a time of light, good music, gift-giving, and joy. And much of it is just that…a season to be jolly! That anticipated season, however, is much too often interrupted in brutalizing ways. It is interrupted by the purveyors of fear and greed in the form of systemic and wholesale violence. We who celebrate Christmas in a serious way cannot fail to take into account those interruptions that are most often perpetrated against the poor, the vulnerable, and most especially children.

The interruption of our good anticipation began long before the Bethlehem story was on our horizon. In the biblical account, the story of violence began with the fearsome work of Pharaoh's pervasive violence upon which his regime depended before that (see Genesis 6:13). Powerful as he was, Pharaoh feared being outnumbered and overwhelmed by his slave-labor force. Acting in his fear, he resolved that all boys born to Hebrew women should be killed (Exodus 1:16). In an irrational act of fear that decimated his own labor force, he commanded:

> Every boy that is born to the Hebrews you shall throw into the
> Nile, but you shall let every girl live (Exodus 1:22).

The fact that the Hebrew midwives outwitted him did not in any way lessen the lethal resolve he articulated.

The narrative of Pharaoh's systemic violence is re-performed by King Herod in Matthew's gospel account. In order to eliminate the threat of the child born in Bethlehem (that fulfilled the prophecy of Micah), Herod ordered the death of all children born in and around Bethlehem:

> He sent and killed all the children in and around Bethlehem
> who were two years old or under (Matthew 2:16).

The fact that the child of Mary escaped (Matthew 2:13-15) does not mitigate the violence of the Judean king. Matthew provides a pathos-filled response to the deathscape of Herod by quoting the prophet Jeremiah:

> A voice was heard in Ramah, wailing and loud lamentation,
> Rachel weeping for her children;
> she refused to be consoled, because they are no more
> (Matthew 2:18; see Jeremiah 31:15).

Mother Rachel, mother of Joseph, mother in Israel, weeps for all the lost children, the ones lost long ago in Egypt, the ones lost to Herod, and in between the ones lost amid the Babylonian exile. Indeed, the Bible is a torrent of grief for lost children who are done in by systemic violence through the managers of greed and fear.

Our time is no less so! Just now we are beset by the indiscriminate death of children in Gaza and Israel. The killing there is unrestrained and no end is in sight. And after Egypt and Babylon and Herod and Gaza and Israel, it will be elsewhere. It will be among us where many children in the US lack protection and support.

We will go on with our light, good music, gift-giving, and joy. But serious celebration of Christmas requires a deep pause to ponder the violence and the children lost. In the end the Christ child prevails…at Easter. But not soon, not easily! Thus Christmas might call for a sober resolve to be at work against systemic violence, at work locally, at work in a practice of generosity, at work shaping policy otherwise. The weeping of Rachel will not soon turn to the laughter of Sarah (see Galatians 4:27; Genesis 21:6). Not soon, not easily! The turn from Rachel's weeping to Sarah's laugh requires active intervention. Thus we might resolve at Christmas that the world becomes a safer place for children, for all those vulnerable to the threat of violence.

www.ingramcontent.com/pod-product-compliance
Lightning Source LLC
Chambersburg PA
CBHW070637030426
42337CB00020B/4058